The Enduring & Everlasting

A PERSONAL STORY OF LOVE TRANSFORMING DEEP GRIEF

LINDSAY STANTON

BALBOA.PRESS

A DIVISION OF HAY HOUSE

Balboa Press books may be ordered through booksellers or by contacting:

Balboa Press
A Division of Hay House
1663 Liberty Drive
Bloomington, IN 47403
www.balboapress.com
844-682-1282

Print information available on the last page.

ISBN: 979-8-7652-4111-0 (sc)
ISBN: 979-8-7652-4112-7 (e)

Balboa Press rev. date: 04/13/2023

Contents

SECTION 2

SECTION 3
How-to Guide to Connection

Foreword

"Be the best person you can be" – RJS

My dad, Roger, was a force. The epitome of strength. He loved every minute of this life. Being Roger's daughter is the greatest joy of my life. My dad was my best friend. We were "2peas in a pod". We were essentially the same person. He taught me to be kind, treat others as you would want to be treated. Always hold your head high and take the high road. To cherish every single day, because it is a gift. He never let a moment go by without telling us he loved us. But he didn't just tell us he loved us. He showed us; every single day. It in was my morning coffees, the notes he'd leave me around the house, just to say he was proud of me. Our country drives in his TR-6 listening to the Bee Gees and watching the sunsets. It was the mornings in middle school when he'd come in my room every morning to help blow dry the back of my hair. It was driving me to preschool while listening to Puff the Magic Dragon and giving me a Lifesaver to get through the day. I could go on and on. I'm forever grateful for the love he gave us and that it will last a lifetime.

I am grateful to have Lindsay. She is a constant, who helps identify signs. It's easy to let our egos block communication.

This is where Lindsay truly thrives. She has not only helped me, but countless others, through their profound grief.

My hope for you is to go forward, while reading Lindsay's words, to remember this life is an extraordinary gift. Our loved ones never truly leave us. They are the essence of everything around us. Love this life of yours and be the best person you can be.

SECTION 1

Our Story

MY STORY — OUR STORY — IS A STORY OF LOVE. PROOF THAT through love death is an illusion, a loss only of our physical body, not our soul.

These are the memories and stories of our love, how my soulmate and I together transcended grief, dimensions, fear, and space to remain connected. I hope our story opens your heart and mind, but mostly your heart, to all of the amazing possibilities and gifts out there just waiting for you to receive them.

I admit I have been incredibly blessed. Long before Roger, the love of my life (lives), my twin flame, became ill I was the recipient of his amazing love. Unconditional, pure love. I often joke that Roger was my number-one fan. He was, he is. All who knew us in business, personally or even through brief encounters, commented about our amazing connection. Our connection was so strong that I am positive others could feel the vibration of energy between us.

I have heard many stories of the accolades, praise, and admiration Roger bestowed on me over the almost 20 years we were together physically, even when I was present. To set the stage properly, I will start with the story of how we met. I will try to tell it as best I can. This story was Roger's favorite and he told it eloquently. I hope I can paint the same beautiful picture with words that he did so often.

The Interview

IT WAS EARLY SUMMER RIGHT BEFORE FOURTH OF JULY 2001. I HAD sent my resume and cover letter for an open sales position at a local sports promotions company, Game Time Promotions. Roger had built the company after years of experience at the likes of P&G, Wilson Sporting Goods (heading up their pro golf division), and Reebok. He had created a fun company that married the promotional industry with sporting goods and well-recognized professional athletes. He had already licensed an impressive roster of athletes. He had a small office and warehouse in the same town where I lived.

At the time I was working full time and getting my master's degree in the city at night. I was scheduled to interview right before heading into Chicago for class. I arrived at the office and found myself accidentally ringing the bell of the warehouse instead of the front office. Every time Roger told this story he took ownership for giving me bad directions. Truth be told, I am not sure this was the case. He always said he was expecting the UPS driver to ring the warehouse bell. Then, with a joyful expression he would say how happy he was to open the door and see me instead. Walking in, I passed shelf after huge shelf of inventory, all these unique products waiting to get boxed and sent to customers. I followed Roger from the warehouse to the front offices.

Many times over the years, he told me that as soon as he opened that warehouse door, he immediately thought "this is the girl of my dreams." He told of how, on that walk from the warehouse up to his private office, he was thinking this deep and sincere thought: "This is the girl I have always wanted, the girl I have dreamt of since I was a little boy, and the opportunity nearly passed me by."

This was a challenging season in Roger's life. He had abruptly lost two of his closest friends. Tony was a highly decorated Vietnam Veteran, a true war hero. Nick was an icon in the music industry, working for Warner Music, signing artists like Prince. Both were golfing buddies with whom he spoke pretty much daily. He spoke so fondly of them, saying Tony was the guy he wanted in his fox hole if shit went down and Nick was the friend who made him laugh, albeit sometimes unintentionally with his golf game.

As if that was not enough heartache and trauma, Roger's dad had been diagnosed with terminal cancer. Roger was facing so much disruption, loss, and change in his life, and now when I walked in the wrong door, he suddenly was faced with all that might have been.

I am convinced, after hearing him tell this story so many beautiful times, he knew. He knew the minute we "met" we had a deep soul connection. He knew our souls recognized each other, were drawn together, and that this was not only what could be, but what *should be* — what the universe planned for our souls many lifetimes before. It was a deep knowing, an instant recognition. In letters to me when we were dating, he chronicled this deep sense of love at first sight. It was instant, snap of the fingers, done.

There was a visceral feeling of belonging and needing to be together. He could always recount every detail of that afternoon: what I was wearing, what was said, and his deep thoughts.

We had a great conversation about the business and his objectives for growth. We discussed which stores he was selling to now, the athletes he worked with, and where he wanted to take the company. I shared my thoughts on potential new opportunities and ways I thought I could contribute. There was a very natural ease to the conversation inconsistent with the average interview. We were both completely comfortable with each other, instantly. We shared a few of our hobbies, running and fitness mostly, and it became clear we were both pretty type-A personalities. He shared an amusing anecdote about the fact that he never used the very large PC behind him at his desk; that was for his assistant. Then, in this state of complete comfort as if we had known each other and been in lockstep for years, he asked about my long-term career goals. Where did I see myself in five years? What was my career plan? Without pause or hesitation, before I could respond or answer, he said: "Because I am worried I could fall in love with you and you will move on."

That conversation rolled through my mind over and over that afternoon for the entire train ride to school, and then on the entire train ride home that night.

And we did fall in love immediately. It was as if we both recognized on some level, not necessarily consciously, that this was our opportunity. The universe had placed us uniquely in the right time and space for this amazing opportunity and we never looked back.

On paper, it might look like this was the most difficult time to start a new relationship, but we just flowed. To the outside world we gave the impression, or thought we did, of slowness, taking it in stride. But for us, truly, it was 160 MPH down an open highway with clear roads ahead as far as our eyes could see.

Roger's love has always been the deepest, truest love I have ever felt. It was like a deep knowing that I was always safe, always in the light, always coveted, and always protected. Unlike any other relationship I'd experience, there were no questions. There was no weighing of pros and cons, no thoughts of our differences or what we had in common, of would this work or was it a waste of time. This was completely different than any experience I ever had. When the person you start dating shows their complete vulnerability the first time you meet by recognizing and verbalizing love for you, it is bound to be different.

Years later, I had a medium describe our connection perfectly. He said: "I get very strong soulmate energy with you two, as if the minute you both met it was like 'Oh, I don't need to talk to anyone else again.'" Exactly, exactly!

Under Our Noses

ROGER'S BUSINESS WAS ONE TOWN OVER FROM WHERE HE LIVED, IN the town where I graduated high school. We had lived in the same town for years and, until the day of my interview had never met or crossed paths in our earthly lives.

It was actually amazing we had not met before that day in 2001. We went to the same gym. This was no mega gym; it started as a very small warehouse type building, only a few rooms, more of a "meathead gym," which certainly wasn't either of us. The gym attracted super serious weightlifters. Roger and I were both very into fitness, but we were not entering any bodybuilding competitions. We were attracted to this little gym for the same reason: serious lifters equaled people who don't bother you while you're trying to work out.

Most gyms have a high contingent of members who are ninety percent there to socialize, ten percent to (sort of) work out. Not Powerhouse; Powerhouse was all business. As a female, this was ideal. I could do my workout and not be bothered. Turns out Roger wanted time to himself working out as well. We had both been going to Powerhouse at close to the same time of day, but for whatever reason, clearly the universe's reason, this was not where we would meet. The gym had expanded to a slightly larger open concept strip mall location. All the cardio equipment was at the front of the gym. Those running or doing any type of cardio were in the path of the entrance and exit, far from those who were there to lift. Roger and I were both very self-motivated fitness people. We didn't need a class, instructor, or coach pushing us; we pushed ourselves enough for an army. Even with the new layout and the fact that there were not that many members, it was not our divine time to meet. The universe had big plans for our entrance into each other's lives.

The crossover didn't stop at the gym. We also discovered we were both pretty serious runners. I ran competitively in high school and college. I was a distance runner, so it made for a little bit easier time staying with it after college.

Much to my college coaches dismay, I ran a marathon with my dad towards the end of my cross-country season. I always loved distance. I never felt like the 5,000- or 10,000-meter races I ran during college were long enough. My coach frequently entered me in both races and it was not unheard of for them to be run on the same day. Roger was one of those relatively rare runners who could pick up and do distance running with little training. Even though he had not run competitively, he started running after college and loved it. He loved the clearing of the head that running provided and the quiet time in nature with just his thoughts.

During one of our first weeks knowing each other, we met on the western trail in our town for a run. We had both often run on this same trail. Months later Roger admitted that he was sucking air a bit trying to keep up on our first run together, as I ran and talked. He joked he was just trying to breathe and not let me know we were going at a faster clip than he was used to. He said we were flying along, and I was barely breathing, just talking away. I can hear his tone as I write this, a little laughter and a little trying to maintain a masculine image. He was so true to who he was, sharing that truth early in our relationship. And not just with me — he joked that he had wondered that day if there was more to my running, only to find out I was a track athlete.

Over the years, he was my running partner. If I was training for a marathon and he wasn't, or if I planned to do more mileage than he cared to do, he would meet me partway. On particularly long runs, we picked a spot to meet on my return, and I ran negative splits, faster back than out, as a test for racing. He always had better speed than me, so he was my perfect rabbit. We typically met up with four miles left on a 16-mile run, and he would help me take seconds or sometimes a minute off of each mile, taking in the evening air, being in nature together. Together was our favorite place to be.

Make A Wish

ROGER WAS THAT RARE PERSON WHO REALLY LIVED LIFE. HE believed, said, and showed that every day is a gift. He said little prayers to himself discreetly each night before bed. He had developed this routine young in life and I always had the impression it was self-taught. Many of his behaviors, routines, and passions were self-taught. He was very much an independent thinker. He never did things because others were doing them.

His closest friends in high school and college often teased him about his independence. As a matter of fact, his fraternity named him the "mystery brother" of the house. This was because he paid his dues and was a member of the fraternity, but never really went to parties. He marched to the beat of his own drum, and it was a damn good drum. With rare exceptions, in the words of old blue eyes Frank Sinatra, he absolutely did it his way. All who knew him had so much respect for this.

Over the years, we had lots of dashboard time together. Whether it was trips from Chicago to Des Moines, to Wateseka to visit his family, or the occasional drive out West, we were often on long car rides together. We even drove occasionally for work trips. Early on in the car on one such trip, Roger did something I've never seen. When the digital dashboard clock flipped to 11:11, he kissed his fingers, touched the digital readout, and said: "It's 11:11, make a wish." I found out it was a frequent practice for him. What I did not connect at the time was the fact that 11:11 is an angel number, and an angel number having significance to Roger made all of the sense in the world. At the time, Roger had three angels on the other side. These angels had crossed over, first his two closest guy friends the year before we met and then the loss of his dad the first year of our union. So much tremendous loss in a short time, especially when you lose people who impact your life daily. I now fully appreciate the context for which the angel number 11:11 came to have such a special meaning for him. Although baptized Catholic and a strong believer in prayer, Roger was more spiritually connected than specifically religious. His spirituality was very strong, felt in so many elements of his life and expressed in how he conducted himself.

He was a very strong believer in the power of the mind. He knew that thoughts matter, and he was certainly influenced by prayer and affirmation. He introduced me to the ideas of Norman Vincent Peale early on. He had read and was a huge proponent of Peale's book *The Power of Positive Thinking*. He never spoke of failure, he never put failure into thoughts or energy, he never put failure out there into the universe at all. He lived the way he believed: stay positive and everything will work out in your favor. These were not just mantras or sayings for him, this was truly the way he lived. It would be a struggle to remember a time when he was down or negative; pretty unusual considering we spent 20 years together on this planet, much of that time working together as well.

Even early in our relationship I witnessed him take on challenges that would break most people. He lived even the most challenging and darkest hours positively. It was deep in him, at a core level, a soul level. And it was contagious. His passion, belief, that you could, you would, we would, accomplish anything was intoxicating. Everyone felt it; people who knew him in any capacity were changed by his positivity.

So many people were influenced by being around Roger, even if it was just a short meeting. I especially noticed this with work, in all of our travels, and the events and meetings we attended. Years later, I often ran into people in our industry, and they commented how much joy they gained from short interactions with Roger. I would hear people comment about his amazing passion for life. People would remember him years, even decades later from a brief encounter. They felt his passion for life at a visceral level. The fact he shared so much hope, passion, and positivity with all he met was a beautiful thing. I am forever thankful to have witnessed it first hand and to hear from others years later. Many people I spoke with after his passing commented how contagious his positivity was and a beautiful reminder to enjoy life, no matter what. He reminded us daily that this specific lifetime we are in is a gift. We are here to live it. Don't wait.

We can all make the wish at 11:11 to carry that way of living forward each day.

Track Team Coming Through

OVER THE YEARS, WORKING TOGETHER IN BOTH THE SPORTING goods and human resources tech space, Las Vegas became a frequent stomping ground for our events and conferences. We were not Vegas material. Neither of us is really drank, we didn't gamble, and we worked out on the daily.

Early in our relationship, within the first few months, we took our first trip to Las Vegas for a trade show. Neither of us had been to there and we had no clue what to expect. This was when I learned that the Vegas hotel rating system is definitely not the same as the rest of the world. We ended up at a hotel (which shall remain nameless) that, trust me, we would never have picked intentionally. We never stayed there again. Despite the hotel, the fact that we did not fit in at all in Las Vegas, and that we were there for work, we had a blast. We got to be together 24/7 and with heavy oxygen pumped into our room and beautiful weather. We enjoyed each other and that was all that mattered. We never complained or felt a certain way about our environment not fitting us. It was our first experience knowing we were at home, no matter where we were, when we were together.

After a few Vegas trade shows, we figured we could make the place conform to us, right? Well, no, but it was worth a shot. Finding a place to work out can be very challenging in

Vegas. The high-end hotels have spas with gyms, as do some of the hotels on the strip, but we did not know this yet. The weather was perfect for being outside.

If you have ever worked a conference or trade show, you know getting to see nature, or even natural light, is a premium, a gift. Generally, you are stuck under bad halogen lights on concrete floors with paper thin carpet from the minute you start the day until you hit the pillow at night.

One late afternoon, we had a lightbulb moment. It was around 75 degrees outside. The sun was out but lowering — the perfect opportunity for a run. We figured it was early enough that there would not be a lot of traffic on the sidewalks. We thought it was too early for people to be drinking and partying, and that we could sneak in a good little run, three to four miles. Welcome to Stanton's Las Vegas newsflash: there are always people on the strip — lots of people. Bold tourists and those selling something to them... everywhere!

This was the first and only run in our lifetime where we were hit with business cards for porn, strippers, and prostitutes. Not exactly your nice trail run. We were teased repeatedly. We had to run up and down every overpass between our hotel and wherever we decided to turn around. On the other hand, because the buildings are so huge, they give the illusion of being much closer together than they actually are, so we ended up going much farther than we realized, and running up and down the stairs and the passageways was a great way to avoid most of the crowds.

We were not discouraged. We were actually amused by this completely unique experience. We talked to the people who tried to hand us cards or asked us what we were doing. We told our stories, chatting with each other about the day and enjoying the fresh air. Then it happened, the moment that put that run in our memory books. A group of fun, young, fit guys saw us coming and cleared the way for us, yelling as they did: "Track team coming through, please, clear the way. Track team coming through!"

We laughed so hard we could barely breathe and run. And it worked. People seemed to think this was some legit thing, that they needed to move aside for us. Of course, many of them might have been drunk or under some other form of influence. As the Stanton track team of two made their way down the Vegas Strip for the first and last time, these guys parted the crowd for us.

The Engagement

FALL 2006, ROGER AND I HAD BOTH TAKEN POSITIONS WITH OTHER organizations, not working together for the first and only time in our relationship. I decided to put my Masters in Public Administration to use and took a job overseeing economic development for a large municipality outside Chicago. Roger had taken a position with an executive search firm in the Chicago suburbs. Our offices were now a good 40 minutes from each other — a big change for us. We loved working together. We were passionate about our careers and work contributions, both high drive over achievers. We loved collaborating, problem solving, and having idea sessions at any point in the day (or night).

When it works well, working together as a couple is a beautiful thing. Having common goals and dreams, and diving into projects can bring you so close, especially if your styles and taste are in line. This was certainly the case for us. Meeting Roger when he hired me was the foundation on which we built our relationship. He allowed me to sell to new, larger department stores; I assisted with product launches and got to work with the famous athletes on our roster. We loved every minute. Each year, we attended large trade shows together in Orlando and Las Vegas for the sporting goods and sporting fashion industries. We checked out the largest launches from athletes, rap stars, and other celebrities. From famous boxers to football players and huge vendors, there were always a lot of balls in the air.

We were in the midst of major culture shock during this period of separation, going from being together 24/7, which we loved, to working in strange new offices with new people where we had no common connection. Being so in love, we made it work. I think deep down we knew the work separation would be temporary.

Roger sent me so many flowers over the two years I was at the city that staff simply assumed any delivery was for me. I saved every card he sent with them, appreciating the special relationship we were blessed to have. He frequently drove 40-plus minutes so we could have lunch together. These weren't fancy lunches, more like bagel sandwiches. We spent our time together trying to make it feel like we were still in the same office. I told him the details of my day, which by his count included five million acronyms from the city (the municipal world loves their acronyms).

Within the first year of this new work situation, we identified an opportunity to work together again. A former contact had a startup and the founder needed help. Roger was asked to assist in what was supposed to be a small role, a small commitment, helping develop a sales plan. He soon found out he was the only one with business expertise, and was asked to assist with more and more of the business.

Personally, we were on track to get married soon. We knew the minute we met we were forever, so there never was a need for conversation, questions, or timelines about our relationship. We always had this deep knowing and confidence in it. Looking back, I see this was incredibly special and unusual.

That same fall, we planned to take a vacation to Rocky Mountain National Park, one of Roger's most cherished spots, filled with meaning and love. Roger had taken his kids there every summer to hike, fish, and attend a camp at the YMCA of the Rockies. We went each summer as well. I had never been on a mountain hike before we met, but instantly fell in love with the experience. The outdoors, fresh mountain smells, intense workouts, and spectacular views won me over immediately.

On our first trip out to Colorado, we were going through the mountains when we called the office to announced we were a couple. We had been careful not to say anything, as it was a new job for me. Now the time was right, since there may have been suspicions about us being on vacation at the same time. It turned out the entire staff was thrilled, thinking all along we would be the perfect couple.

We went to Colorado every summer, usually in July or August, when the weather was perfect and the snow had melted for the long hikes we liked to tackle. We had already done our summer trip, but Roger suggested another one in late fall, often the start of winter in the mountains. I'm not going to lie — I was curious as to why we were going then, and even had my suspicions about a possible proposal. I actually tried to do a little recon mission before we left, to see if anyone would tell me, but of course no one did.

Next there was the box. We generally shipped a box of supplies out to the YMCA before we left: fishing supplies, extra clothes, etc. Given the time of year, we sent a good-sized box ahead, so I was convinced if there was a ring it must be in the box. One morning, after we arrived, Roger ran to the lodge to get something. That was my opportunity! I searched every inch of that box, pockets, fly fishing belts, etc. No ring, so I gave up. I knew he didn't have the ring on him while flying out to Colorado because we'd carried on our bags as we always did, and he was searched randomly at TSA. The TSA agent went through his briefcase in great detail, along with his carry on, and took out many items right in front of me. His briefcase was practically empty by the time the agent was done. I *knew* there was no ring and figured this wasn't going to be the engagement trip after all.

The second day, we decided to go on a hike — one of Roger's favorite hikes to take with the kids. It was a simple, short hike, no need for backpacks or a bunch of gear, just our standard hiking shoes and clothes. The hike is about five miles round trip, and on our way up trailhead it started to snow. In the mountains, the snow is very pretty, but the snowflakes are big and heavy. They cover both you and the ground really fast. We did not have snowshoes or extra gear.

As we got close to the top of this very pretty hike that now had become a beautiful winter wonderland, the mountain rocks were completely covered in snow. I caught the edge of a large flat, smooth rock with my left boot just the right way and went down like a slingshot. I did not get hurt at all, but Roger insisted he take the lead after that.

We got to the top of the trailhead covered in dewy snow, taking in the gorgeous views. That's when he knelt down and proposed. On the way back I asked, totally perplexed, how did he have the ring. I rehashed the security play-by-play and, true-confessions style, told of my sneaky ways with the box. The TSA agent, a very young guy, had been swayed by Roger. When he grabbed Roger's briefcase, Roger leaned in and whispered about the ring and told him, no matter what, *do not* take out that box. The young agent, probably slightly terrified, obliged. For me, it was perfection. That incident with TSA absolutely convinced me no proposal was happening on this trip, making the actual proposal a total surprise.

In perfect yin and yang, balance-of-the-universe fashion, our engagement story does not end there. We went down the mountain ecstatically, so happy, laughing at my confession. Roger was super proud that he totally surprised me. He was leading and I'll be damned if he didn't go down in the exact same spot I had. The spot was completely recovered in fresh new snow. Thankfully, he did not get hurt either, but we sure did have a story. We laughed so hard at his "no, no I'm leading on the way back. I know where to step, just follow me." Perfect ending to the beautiful beginning of the glorious ebbs and flows of our soul connection.

Ball Buster

GIVEN WE WERE BOTH COLLEGE ATHLETES AND SERIOUSLY INTO fitness, Roger and I loved to compete. I was a track and cross-country athlete; Roger was a golf athlete. On the surface, the two sports don't seem like they have a lot of commonalities, but both golf and track are sports where it's all you and your performance for your team. There is no hiding, there is no ducking behind other team members. You leave it all on the course or on track, and everyone sees what you brought that day.

Although golf is a skills game and track is more of a natural sport, they both require physical ability and a really strong mind. In many ways, both are a battle of wills. In golf, you take each shot one at a time and let go of whatever bad shot or hole you played before. You clear your head, step up, and hit like it was the first opportunity of the day. With running, you have to let your mental strength force you through when your body screams "uncle, uncle, uncle." You push through for that next mile, breaking it down into achievable segments, your mind telling you "you've got this!" Roger was a runner, too. Running, like golf, requires some natural abilities; either you've got great VO2 (maximal oxygen capacity) or you don't. Either you've got great hand-eye coordination, or you don't. The rest you can learn with practice, repetition, and grinding it out.

These are the mindsets we both brought to our relationship. A drive-hard, challenges-are-fun, we-can-beat-the-odds, we've-got-this way of thinking. We both loved to push ourselves mentally and physically. And we loved even more that we were truly a team when we had the opportunity to accomplish something together.

This was why we loved hiking in the mountains, particularly at high altitude. It was a team effort: from choosing our food and snacks, hitting the grocery store for supplies as we rolled into town, and strategically packing our large backpack. It was so much a team effort that we did not carry separate backpacks. We packed one pack and shared carrying it. It was common for the person carrying the pack not to want to give it up. While it's not fun carrying an overloaded pack filled with six to ten liters of water, two changes of clothes, snacks, lunch, and often fishing gear, we wanted to make life easier for each other. This was how we did things. We loved it. Hiking gave us many things we loved: alone time, team building, time in nature, and awesome physical experiences.

In our early days going to Rocky Mountain National Park, we frequently fished with one of Roger's closest friends, Joe. Joe had a fly-fishing shop at the YMCA. He offered guided hike and fishing trips, often with families. Joe always took us on hikes, and we loved to fish with him. We always set aside at least one evening for fly fishing.

Fly fishing at night is magical. You have the majestic mountains all around you, the cool crisp evening mountain air, and the sky, which is absolutely stunning. Looking at the moon and the stars with the mountains at elevation, you cannot help but feel connected to all life, the universe, and the source. You set up at dusk to be ready when evening hits. When the sun sets and the moon shows in the night sky, flies start hitting the ponds. The night's light reflects on the water and the trout start jumping. Just watching the flies and fish pop is fun. Night fly fishing can be a wonderful opportunity to catch "whales."

Joe knew all the best spots to hike and fish in the Rockies. He helped us plan many a hike over the years. These outings were a huge treat; the entire day was an experience. Early in the morning, we ran to the famous Donut Haus, *the* stand for coffee and donuts, to start the day. We always wanted to hit the trail really early for a long hike. Even the car ride to our destination was an experience with Joe, listening to whatever hip mix of tunes he put together just for Roger. Each trip was special.

Mid-morning on the first day of this particular trip, we hit Joe's shop. We had taken a trail map from the lodge and found a great trailhead off the beaten path, one we'd hiked before. This hike had great switchbacks at the start and a nice trailhead a little ways into the park, which translated to fewer people on it, making it much more peaceful. We pulled out our map and laid it on the glass counter. We told Joe we were thinking of Lake Ypsilon. Our eager beaver vibe filled the air of the old school YMCA building. Joe looked at us with a slightly shocked expression and said: "No. Rog you don't want to do that. Ypsilon is a total ball buster." We looked at each other with huge smiles, knowing what the other person was thinking. He could not have said anything that would have sealed the deal faster and tighter than that.

That day started our annual Ypsilon tradition. One time while we were hiking, someone had to be airlifted out. Another time we had to give two guys water because they were not prepared for the difficult hike. Ypsilon is an enchanted forest. That hike always provided us an opportunity to bond with each other and with nature; to get back to what mattered. It made us feel centered, knowing we always had each other in such a special way.

The forest there is different than anywhere I've experienced. It is so high up. There are quite a few seriously vertical portions, in addition to the steady climb up throughout the hike. Getting to the lake is hard. With very limited exposure to humans, the trail and forest are pristine and beautiful. We always saw gorgeous flowers along the edge of the trail, Indian paintbrush, and other red, purple and yellow flowers I never saw while hiking anywhere else.

One year we went up in early July and it had been a year with really heavy snow, so as we went up, we actually hit sections of several feet of snow rapidly melting down the mountain, creating many streams on the trail. We saw a stunning snowshoe hare in the grass who was still in his winter attire — the most gorgeous rabbit we'd ever seen. We were probably the only people he had ever encountered, and he had no problem letting us take a few admiring photos from the path as he watched us with interest.

To get to the lake, you have to hike down along the edge of a small waterfall next to the trail. The fall is perfectly thin and seeps into a small creek working its way down the mountain to the lake. You go down then climb up again, which makes the return really challenging (or you could use "less than fun") to get out. At the lake, the mountains are reflected on the water all around you — you are literally surrounded by mountains. The views are unbeatable.

Once there, we would take a break for lunch and lay absorbing the mountain sun and recharging before the trip out. We never brought waders on that hike, they are too heavy, so we walked out on the large boulders to get as far into the lake as we could so Roger could fish. He fished along the edges, moving from edge to edge along the inlets, working the pools of fish. They were often hidden, tucked away in small spots he had to find.

Eating even a simple peanut butter and jelly sandwich is next level after that hike. You think you're having a five-star meal. Every year at Ypsilon, a not-so-shy, very adorable, little marmot visited us. Like th snowshoe hare, he was not intimidated by us at all. We loved seeing him. He seemed most interested in scoring some of our snacks. He would try and be so stealth creeping up to our backpack as we fished and get braver and braver as we ate lunch. It was the icing on the cake of our beautiful ball-buster hike.

The Wedding

WE DECIDED TO GET MARRIED IN SPRING 2007. WE WERE MAKING plans to sell both of our houses and buy "our" house, which required coordination, along with multiple types of storage units.

We knew as soon as we met we were meant to be together and would be married. That deep knowing made our engagement and wedding planning calmer than most. We debated the details, the how, the where, and the when. Our immediate and extended family and friends were all excited about the engagement. I remember my grandmother really wanting to be part of the wedding or after party. She wasn't sure how long she had, so she hoped we would get married quickly after the proposal.

Ultimately, we tuned out everything and everyone, and listened to our inner voices that led to us get married in Saint Croix. We decided a destination wedding, as it's commonly termed, was the way for us to go, but with two caveats: the ceremony would be just us, but it was going to be all in — clearly a wedding. What I mean is it wasn't going to be a Las Vegas wedding chapel type of deal; we would have a traditional, real ceremony. We were wedding our soulmates, so it had to be all us and one hundred percent a real wedding.

We had a professional photographer, a gorgeous wedding cake, and beautiful and brilliant colored island flowers. I had my hair and makeup done and wore a full-on wedding dress. Roger wore a full-on tux.

Our minister was a beautiful soul, very into animal rescue, who had lived on the island all her adult life. She and I had lunch the day before while Roger snuck in an extra round of golf. We got to know each other, and it validated that she was the perfect fit for our vows — a very kind, caring person — the perfect minister to help join us together officially.

When you travel outside of the continental United States for a wedding, one thing that can be easily forgotten is your marriage certificate and the need to follow the requirements of that country and location. I'd heard stories about destination wedding challenges, so this was top of mind with me. I sent in all of the certified paperwork and payment information required for our license. We knew we would fly in and go to get our marriage license the next day, which would then need to be signed by our minister following our ceremony. I had called the office and confirmed all of the details the week prior. The day before our wedding, we took a cab to the city office to pick up our license. We provided our names and explained why we are there. Three or four people working there proceeded to run around, disappear, run around some more, disappear, and run around some more, for what felt like forever. A man came out, looking all official, explaining that they couldn't find our paperwork. As panic set in, I explained I had called and verified everything the week before. He apologized, but definitely started heading down the path of us not getting our license that day. I was getting visibly upset at this point. Roger and I stepped outside to talk briefly to our driver — the cab had been waiting for us, as we thought it would be a quick in and out, 10 minutes tops.

We told the driver there was an issue and asked if he could please wait. Roger went back alone, and I can only imagine what he said. What I know is he walked out with our marriage certificate and a new friend. Crisis averted. I asked him on the ride back to the resort what he had said to make things happen; he said he had pleaded how much it meant for us to be official tomorrow and could they please make this happen for us — for his soon-to-be wife.

The wedding day was perfect — official and perfect. We were married a few hundred yards from our wedding suite at the resort, in a historical landmark sugar mill. The suite was set up with a separate room closed off so the bride could get ready without the groom seeing her.

It was a midday ceremony, with sun shining on us as it hovered over the ocean. We stood at the edge of that mill surrounded by beauty and filled with love. The mill was a beautiful stone structure with large openings on every side overlooking the ocean. The round "windows" in the sugar mill let in the sun and ocean breeze while we said our vows. It was the best day to get married to the best man in the world. Souls always and forever connected, that connection permanently inscribed in our rings.

Roger always laughed at the fact that 30 minutes after our ceremony we were in casual clothes, I in a cute sun dress and he in nice slacks, enjoying the evening, relaxed and having a beautiful seafood dinner overlooking the ocean.

Just us, golf, and the ocean. We wouldn't dream of it any other way.

Cheerleaders

ON THE RARE OCCASION ROGER WENT FLY FISHING IN JACKSON Hole without me, he always made Diana feel special on his trip. After putting in a full day on the water and trying to keep up with work obligations in between casts, he took Diana out to at least one dinner. The topics at these dinners covered everything from current events, politics, news, and their favorite topic, from what they both separately shared with me — their love for me. The two of them were completely in sync on current events and politics. Diana loved having someone to talk to who was just as passionate as she was. As a daily connoisseur of the *Wall Street Journal* and CNN, Roger fit the bill.

Diana always called after these dinners to tell me all the details of the amazing meal they enjoyed. As a former professional chef, she loved the artistry of being presented a wonderful meal at a nice restaurant. Her descriptions always included how handsome Roger looked and how much she appreciated being taken out by my kind, dapper husband. She detailed exactly what he wore — how he cleaned up from his day in Orvis gear just to take her to dinner. Her accounts showcased what these outings meant to her. She adored time with Roger and always shared their talk of me. I'm partially convinced the two of them loved each other out of a mutual intense love for me.

Never in my life have I had such amazing support, warmth, and unconditional love. Roger was by far my number one fan. My cheerleader. I am beyond blessed! Diana proudly wore the cheerleader hat as well. They had a totally unique way of making me feel so loved, so good about who I am, without any fakeness or airs. I never had to pretend, embellish, or be anything but authentically myself with the two of them. With both Roger and Diana, I knew this deep within me as soon as we met. They were and are my number one fans. Today I continue to do everything I can to make sure they are proud, to represent the qualities within me they talked about most, knowing they are cheering me on from the other side.

Just Pay the Bill

IN THE WINTER OF 2012, ROGER HAD HIS HIP REPLACED. HIS FIRST hip replacement, to be accurate. He was so great at sales he almost ended up with two hip replacements being done at once. Thankfully for me and his daughter, Meghan, this didn't happen. I remember him suggesting it multiple times to the top orthopedic doctor at Rush Hospital, who we visited him multiple times in preparation for surgery. One of the top surgeons in the country, he was working on quite a few athletes in the NFL, NBA, and MLB. Because Roger presented the idea of the double replacement with such confidence, the team went along with it and actually had him listed for bilateral hip replacement.

When you undergo hip replacement, you completely rely on your good hip — your good side — while recovering. With a full hip replacement, they have you up and walking in less than 24 hours. Roger was actually walking stairs at the hospital the morning after his surgery. They don't mess around. The last thing they want are patients to get blood clots or form scar tissue from non-usage.

I remember going down for the last consultation prior to Roger's surgery. They went over all of the details of what to expect during surgery and recovery, and had us set up the physical therapy, which would start as soon as he got home from the hospital. Towards the end of the appointment, Roger paused and said: "Hey Doc, what do you think? Is the bilateral the best way for me to go?"

The doctor looked at him seriously, then with a half grin said: "Well I'm so glad you finally asked! No!"

Roger looked floored, clearly unaware that his sales job almost led to a total debacle with recovery. So, chart changed — single left hip surgery coming up! The second hip would be scheduled when he was fully recovered from the first surgery. Roger rocked recovery, but unfortunately had a bad reaction to the pain medication and had to wean off of them very quickly. Neither of us took so much as Advil for pain, and I think Roger was motivated to get back to being fully functional. He did not want to rest, and certainly did not want to miss what was going on with the company.

The winter of 2012 was not typical. It was the year a huge snowstorm trapped hundreds of cars on Lakeshore drive. That was the day before Roger's first hip surgery. We had even gone down to the hospital the night before just to be safe. We figured we would grab a nice dinner on our way downtown. We stopped in Oakbrook, about halfway to the city, and looked for a restaurant. Due to the crazy storms, there was only one restaurant open, and we were the only people in it except the staff.

Two days after his release from the hospital, I had him all set up at home watching the Golf Channel and was going to run out and pick up dinner. The streets were totally clear by now. I drove downtown, pulled into the city building, but didn't realize until way too late that they had used the city parking lot as a dump zone for all the extra snow. I barely pulled in, but the front of my front wheel drive car, a sedan, was completely stuck. First I tried calling my stepdaughter, Meghan, then my dad (he has trucks). No luck. I then called Roger *only* so he could call his buddy, our neighbor and the

---

Lindsay Stanton

builder of our house, because I knew he had a truck with a hitch. He agreed to call Arnie. When I hung up, Meghan called back and started to head my way. I called Roger back to see if he had any luck getting ahold of Arnie. As soon as he answered, I could tell he was in the car. Roger drove a Mercedes CLS550, about the lowest car to the ground you can get and not exactly a winter vehicle. He just had his hip replaced. He had not even migrated past wearing pajamas and was only two days home from the hospital.

Me on the call with him: "Where are you?"

Roger mumbled something, not wanting to fess up.

Meghan pulled in to the parking lot and I could now also see Roger's car. Full marks for him being chivalrous. He knew I needed help and, as with every time I was in need, he had me covered. Meghan and I were totally freaked out, though. Both of us had visions of him getting out and slipping on the ice or snow and having to go back for more surgery. Meghan and I instinctively and immediately flanked him; I had his left side, she had his right, as we guided him into the back seat of the car somewhat reclined and took him home. The neighbor came and got my car. When things settled down and it was just the two of us, I realized Roger was wearing jeans. I asked him *how* he get his PJs off and his jeans on. He told me he had gone upstairs — a very large flight of stairs — to our primary closet, slipped the PJs off while half laying on the floor, and shimmied into the jeans. I asked him what he thought he was going to do when he got to me, and he said — so innocently — go get help. So sweet. I could have gotten help, but it was so important to him to take care of me, provide for me in my time of need that he instinctively abandoned all self-protective instincts and normal reason. As crazy as it was, it was such a beautiful display of selflessness and unconditional love.

Mateo

IN THE WINTER OF 2011, MY FIRST, ORIGINAL HEART DOG WAS A little over 12 years old. We had found a cancerous tumor by his left hip that we caught really early and, luckily, were able to have the tumor surgically removed. We also did chemotherapy as a precaution to make sure we got all of the cancerous cells. Chemo for dogs is not nearly as hard on them as it is on us. He never even got sick during the few weeks of treatment. We got to have almost two more years with him as a result. They were a great, healthy two years with lots of walks, play, and love. Dante was the first major loss I ever experienced. In retrospect, it taught me many things. The loss of Dante helped me face all that was to come 10 years later. Another enormous first for me was my first knowledge of experiencing a dream visitation. I had several with Dante, but one came within a few days of his passing, when I was so deep in grief that I cried until I drifted into a nap. He visited me, giving me a deep knowing that he was okay, he was still with me. It was as if he was opening the door in my mind for the many, many signs I was to receive in the next months and years to follow.

Dante was very intuitive and extremely emotionally in tune. I know most dogs are sensitive to sadness, pain, and even our health problems, but Dante had extreme powers in this area, even as a puppy. When he was only 10 weeks old or so, I was dealing with horrible debilitating fibroids. He was just a puppy, but he would lay with me for hours. He did not jump around or beg to go out, he just laid peacefully with me, knowing that's exactly what I needed.

When Roger and I were dating, his family and friends commented how Dante and I were a package deal. I took Dante on walks and errands — car rides to the stores that allowed him. He was my canine soul partner. Not surprisingly, I faced a depression when he transitioned out of the physical world. Also not surprising, he quickly sent me signs to let me know all was well. After a few months and several dream visitations with him, he started sending me other signs and messages about my future canine partner. He sent me visions and messages leading up to one of our annual summer trips to Rocky Mountain National Park. They were images and thoughts of a Spinone puppy related to him. I had bred him when he was younger.

Often when we went to Estes Park, Roger and I visited Madame Vera, a resident psychic who has a space at the famous, supposedly haunted Stanley Hotel. It seems amusing, but she is actually a very, very good intuitive and I have always enjoyed our sessions. Many times, she mentioned very specific events and upcoming things in our lives. It became a bit of a ritual on our visits, and we had fun talking with her. Her readings accurate and we always engaged with her, enjoying her energy and conversation. She was very aligned with us and was a big animal lover as well.

On our annual visit in the summer of 2012, she immediately tuned into Dante's energy. He was communicating through her, which was the first time I had this type of experience and I started to get a bit of an understanding of how it works. I guess Roger did as well, though he did not seem at all surprised. She told us how Dante was sending another dog, the same breed, and that the dog was going to be a he. And *he* was going to be related to Dante. Of course she didn't even know I had bred Dante, or any information about his lineage. She described this puppy in detail. Dante was brown roan, a beautiful color combination — a brown body with flecks of light/white throughout the coat, and he had velvety dark brown ears. Nestled into the top of his gorgeous brown crown was this beautiful white crest that stood out so handsomely.

Madame Vera described how the puppy would have the same head crest, but his body was going to be light in color. She went on to describe in detail how he would be at the "big dog show in New York that's always on TV" and how everyone in the breed would know him. She said he would get all of this recognition. "He is going to strut his stuff big time!" Without knowing it, she was describing a show dog — a top show dog. After the session, Roger turned to me, knowing the other signs I had been receiving as well, and said get your Spinone. As soon as we got to the car I called Diana, not only my best female friend but also a Spinoni breeder, to tell her the story. If you know dogs and dog breeding — rare breeds especially — you know you can wait years for a puppy. Rare breeds mean a limited numbers of breeders and limited number of lines, which can mean extra-long wait times for puppies. I had no idea if Diana knew of a breeding planned anytime soon.

As soon as I told her we were in the market, she told me the day before she had decided to breed her beautiful female import from Italy, Onda, one last time. And she had decided to breed her with Dante's grandson. She knew nothing of Madame Vera's reading; she had made that decision the day before and I had no idea. And the breeding would happen quickly, as Onda was about ready.

On August 15, 2012, our puppy was born, along with eleven brothers and sisters. Our little guy was the first born. Diana said she knew as soon as he was born that he was the one for us. Over the months leading up to the puppies birth, I felt very drawn to a specific name, Mateo. Mateo is the Italian version of Matthew, which means gift from God. The meaning of names is very important to me; when I am selecting them I tend to do a lot of research. Dante means the enduring, the everlasting, my everlasting gift from above. During those months I had so many amazing signs of validation of the name Mateo. Once I was set on it, I shared my idea with Roger, and he loved it. We had so many messages and signs about Mateo from random places: at work on a production set, while traveling, you name it, we were hearing the name Mateo. Dante and the universe were bringing Mateo to us. And Mateo's personality was exactly what I needed to help me heal. As serious as Dante was, Mateo was the clown. He was very intuitive as well, but always made us laugh, and he was so full of himself with a big, big personality.

Almost a year after our visit with Madame Vera, I hadn't really thought about her comment about dog shows, but it just so happened that the Spinoni National Specialty Week was upon us. The National is the one time when members of a specific breed get together and compete with one another. It is a big deal, especially with a rare breed like Spinoni, when getting good numbers for competition can be more challenging. The National fell right after Mateo was about to turn six months old, which is the minimum age to compete in a dog show.

I thought, why not? Let's see what happens. What happened was he won — he won every time he went in the ring that weekend. Every time he showed, he got a ribbon, and even more important, he loved it. He was the biggest ham. The crowd loved him, and he ate it up and just performed more. The first time he ever went into the ring he won a dog toy. Before our handler could grab it from the judge, Mateo did, and he carried it all the way around the ring.

People were cheering and laughing. He went on to qualify for Westminster — "the big dog show in New York on TV" — every year he was on the show circuit. Mateo became the top-ranking dog in the breed throughout history for breed points. He won top honors countless times. Dante showed us the way and helped us, enabling us to hear directly through Madame Vera. Mateo turn out to be our gift from God, and I credit all of what occurred for truly opening me up to the possible. The knowing, the trust, the magic. Divine timing, divine assistance, and divine love.

Jackson Hole

ON OUR FIRST TRIP TO JACKSON HOLE IN 2012, WE FELL COMPLETELY in love with Wyoming. What's not to love? The spot was like coming home for us. We flew in looking at the Tetons, an absolutely stunning view. Even the airport was beautiful — small, intimate, everyone knows everyone — not to mention the gorgeous antler arch that greeted us as we walked off the runway. The airport is designed primarily for private planes with limited commercial terminals, so we walked right off the runway.

Jackson Hole is a truly mystical place. One visit and we were hooked. The mountains, the hiking, the scenery, the people, the food, and the vibe was one hundred percent us. The icing on the mystical cake was Diana — my best female friend, second mother, and part of my soul family — who lived just over the pass. When Roger and I first started dating, Diana moved from the Chicago burbs to Driggs, over the Jackson Hole pass on the Idaho side. The drive through the pass from Wyoming to Idaho is gorgeous, winding through downtown up into the mountains to the top of the pass, where the views are incredible.

Our first trip there was a work trip, sponsored by Comcast, our client and partner at the time. They were promoting a new show about to launch on FX that had been filmed in Jackson

Hole. They put us up in an amazing resort where they had housed the cast and crew during filming. The resort was perched at the peak of the mountain with insanely picturesque views. Just walking out and smelling the crisp, clean air was a gift.

Diana had set Roger up to fish with the top angler company in the area. Her twin brother, who had passed a few years before, had been an avid fly fisherman and outdoors lover. He had fallen in love with the area, as well with the amazing trout in Wyoming and Idaho. All trout fishing is catch and release, of course. These breath-taking fish in all their glory have several peak seasons in the Jackson Hole/Idaho area, making it a fly fisher's euphoria. Roger came back sharing stories and photos of the day, pictures of the most gorgeous brown, rainbow, and cutthroat trout, some of them "whales" as the fishermen refer to them. I remember Roger's love and fascination with the endless barley fields they drove past to get to their special fishing spot. The best anglers always have secret spots. Often these spots require long drives and treks with waders, but ask any who loves the sport, and they will tell you it is well worth the work. Plus, the challenging terrain makes the secret spot less likely to be discovered.

After that first trip, we went back every year, always in conjunction with spring or fall fly hatch so Roger could experience prime fishing. One year we even did a doubleheader. For us non-baseball people, that meant Jackson Hole for a few days then straight to Colorado and our annual summer vacation spot. On one of our trips to Jackson Hole, in fall 2018, things got very interesting. We flew in just in time to get for a gorgeous round of golf before sundown, watching the blazing sun slide down the mountain peak as we finished our round, then off to dinner and a visit with Diana. She had just lost one of her precious canine kids and was not feeling up to a full outing. The next day we did our morning drive to

Henry's Fork Anglers, the fly-fishing shop where Roger always booked his guided fishing trips. I dropped Roger off with Tom, his favorite guide in Wyoming/Idaho. I rode with him to the shop and hung out while they packed lunches, loaded the truck, and hooked up the trailer. Then I drove back to spend the day with Diana, loving on her and the pups. Roger sent me photos of fish, great shots of him on the boat, and the beautiful surroundings. Fly fishing can make for a long day between hiking, wading, balancing in the boat, and potentially bringing in a whale, if you get lucky. You get your workout in.

This particular day, while Roger's guide drove him back to the resort, I got ready for a romantic dinner in the mountains. While Roger got ready, I suddenly felt something was wrong. I started itching at a level and intensity I have never experienced, then my face started to feel weird. I knocked on the bathroom door and told Roger I thought something was wrong. He opened the door with a look of shock. It was shock for both of us, as I was in anaphylactic shock. I had never in my life had an allergic reaction to anything, yet there I was in full blown anaphylaxis in the middle of the mountains, a good 40 miles from any hospital.

Roger owned emergencies. He didn't panic. He knew instantly exactly what to do. In our approximately 17 years together at that point, we had never experienced or talked about or even mentioned allergic reactions. But he managed the situation like an expert. He got a Benadryl pack from the front desk, found out how far the hospital was, and determined it was in our/my best interest for him to drive me, rather than risk waiting for an ambulance. I'm sure he created a record that day — 140 mph in a rental Chevy Malibu.

As we flew down the country road to the closest hospital, he knew driving like Batman was as important as keeping calm. By that point, the swelling of my mouth, tongue, and nose had significantly restricted my breathing. I knew this could take me out, but there was no way that was going to happen on Roger's watch. His calm, confident demeanor kept me settled. I am sure he was not calm at all on the inside, but he never let me see it. He got me into the hospital and he stopped everyone to get me instant attention. A few IVs later, everything settled down quickly. Although the swelling in my face lasted a day or so, the scary stuff was over. We never did find out the cause, but thanks to Roger that was not my day to leave my "earth suit," in the words of Gary Zukoff. The night ended at the last bar and restaurant open in town, with us laughing over a very late-night dinner.

Black Cats and Seat Belts

STARTING AROUND 2013, WE WERE HEAVILY FOCUSED ON BUILDING technology and partnerships for our company and our travel really kicked up. I was in charge of our partnerships and speaking engagements. Roger had asked me to be the face of the company, working with media and at events.

When building a new brand, specifically in a market where the other vendors in the space spend millions of dollars in advertising, you need to be creative to get recognized. This is especially important when you are bringing a "blue ocean" product or solution to market. "Blue Ocean" is the ability to bring a new product to market regardless of if there is heavy competition or no competition and do something / offer something in a unique way that has never been done before. We were doing just that. We were very strategic in driving awareness, including having partners feature us in their very pricey sponsored booths. We featured our products with a mini production set and had our film crew showoff who we were. Showing up with top-notch equipment and quality production was a conversation starter. Just like becoming a recognized thought leader in the space, it helped drive market recognition.

No one wants to buy when they are being sold aggressively. If you can show how you can help them and show you are knowledgeable about solutions that can solve their challenges, you have a win and people listen to you. That led to our strategy.

First, we hit major media outlets. Every month, job numbers are released in the US. Major news outlets, like CNBC, MSNBC, and Fox, need help communicating these numbers to their viewers and listeners. They want to communicate the numbers and the trends the numbers show, as well as the details of what those numbers potentially mean to their audience. For example, are all sectors growing or only certain sectors? What are good fields to go into if you are looking for a job? What education track would be best? You get the picture. This is all relevant to those consuming their media, including their advertisers.

Step one was getting on as many outlets as possible, building credibility as an expert. We used the data we as a company were seeing across our global customer base, and there was a lot of great data, providing valuable information to the media and, therefore, the public. A feature on Forbes or CNBC is a great entrée for a lot of things that help market your company, including industry speaking engagements. This was the first step,

The next was to get HR technology and recruiting event speaking engagements. We submitted to the large associations and recognized industry events. I was selected a lot, to the tune of 12 to 15 speaking engagements a year from 2013 to 2019. Remember, these speaking engagements were not really my "day job;" more of a side hustle, a way to facilitate engagement. When I/we were not headed to the latest conference or industry event, I was trying to secure global partnerships and clients.

Anyone who travels frequently for work knows if you've seen one hotel or conference center, you've seen them all. And that is likely all you'll see. That was fine by me. Unlike most business travelers, I had the rare gift of frequently getting to travel with the love of my life and best friend, Roger. Game changer.

On the rare occasions Roger wasn't with me, I tried to make the trip as quick as the event allowed. This was best for me personally and practically for the business, as well, since there was plenty to do at home base.

Around February 2013, I had one of these in-and-out trips. I was going to Orlando for a speaking engagement and meetings with our head of sales at the time. She was going in ahead of me from the East Coast so I could do a quick turn around and she would handle the bulk of the meetings with another salesperson. I am not a fan of Orlando in general for business travel, but you can multiply that feeling by one hundred when you send me there in spring break season, exactly when I was going on this particular trip. I had a certain feeling of dread going into this trip that went beyond a normal spring break timed trip to Orlando, with a million kids at TSA. I just did not want to go, which was rare because traveling was second nature at this point. I didn't want to go while packing. I didn't want to go when the car service came to pick me up. I didn't want to go while feeling like a zombie at TSA at four o'clock in the morning. There was just a generally shitty vibe going into the trip. I was pouting and practically crying — again rare —about the entire deal. One redeeming factor, we had wi-fi in flight, which meant I could keep occupied, including sending emails and texting Roger.

Another not-so-great thing about flying to Orlando in early spring are the storms over the Panhandle. The majority of our flight was extremely turbulent; we were rocking pretty good. This was the rockiest flight for the longest duration I have ever experienced. At one point the flight crew announced they would not be leaving their seats and not to hit the call button unless you were "having a heart attack or a major medical emergency." This was followed by something I have not heard before or since in all my years of travel: "We aren't sure what is going to happen." At this point I messaged Roger: "I love you."

A few moments later I hit the call button and wow if the flight attendant's eyes could have thrown darts. "Are you having medical emergency?" he asked/yelled. "No, but a black cat just walked under my seat." He looked at me like I was insane. Then a man yelled: "Oh my God, my cat jumped out of the bag under my seat." The flight crew was now crawling on the floor, bouncing around, trying to get this cat back to its "seat."

Yeah, this trip had bad energy!

The return trip was a moderate improvement. The same horrible storms plagued the entire flight home. A huge snow and rainstorm hit the Midwest while we were enroute. We could see the snow and lightning while the pilots tried to navigate proper elevation for the smoothest ride possible. It was like a Hummer driving off road in the mountains. I was watching the flight tracker while messaging with Roger about what he thought based on the weather on the ground in Chicago. I wanted to know if we're going to make it back into Chicago or hit the storm and have to land.

I wanted to get home to see him, of course, but I also had an important meeting with a big potential partner the next afternoon in Chicago. We were over Ohio by now, so I started to feel good about our chances of getting to Midway. I didn't realize we had already circled and were moving away from Chicago. The pilot came on and said we were being rerouted from Midway to Columbus, Ohio. This was my first experience with a diversion, so I didn't know the deal. You're basically screwed. Once you have landed safely, you are no longer the airline's problem, period. Good luck to you.

Not knowing this, I was hopeful, mostly because as we were landing the pilot told us we might be able to combine our flight with another that had been diverted and get one plane into Midway. Maybe they would let that one plane land. They said we could wait on the plane if we wanted, but if we got off, we couldn't get back on. I called Roger to see what he thought I should do. He told me to get off the plane and run to the car rental He would call and book me a car. "There's no way you're getting out of there by air tonight," he said. "And likely not tomorrow, either, based on the weather here."

I grabbed my carry-on from the overhead and sprinted to the car rental. Roger called while I was running to tell me he had rented me the last all-wheel drive they had. Now I just had to drive through snow, rain, sleet, and ice from Columbus to Chicago. I was so thankful for my man's quick thinking and reaction, always clutch in a critical situation.

Run Boston Run

ON AN EARLY DECEMBER DAY IN 2015, ROGER AND I DID A QUICK turnaround trip to snowy Boston, packing as many things into a 48-hour business trip as possible.

In less than two days, we met with our corporate attorney, who frequently told us "you need to write a book," as well as one of the largest recruitment agencies in the world, and still managed to get in an amazing seafood dinner and see one of our investors. We stayed at our favorite hotel in the heart of downtown. The Westin Copley is not my favorite hotel because it is super posh or the highest end. Don't get me wrong, it is very nice, but it is my favorite hotel in Boston because it is in the heart of everything: the cobble stone streets, brownstones, and unique shops that make up downtown. I have walked every road within a two-mile radius of Copley, taking in every boutique, district shop, and restaurant while plowing through my daily step goal.

This particular trip was memorable, though, not because of the gorgeous brownstones or walking the historical city, or even the exciting meetings we had. This trip got its grit at Boston Logan Airport.

We got through TSA in a rush. I had a conference call with a manager at our partner Adecco. This particular manager was the bane of my professional existence. Any time it would be particularly challenging for me to have a call with him was exactly when he *urgently* required my attention. He would dangle the proverbial carrot of more business, so of course I would move heaven and earth (okay, maybe just pick the fast lane at security and make sure my liquids were out of my bag), to speak with him.

Rushing through TSA, Roger and I managed to find a quiet space, slightly hidden, and as close to the gate as we could. I got on the phone with my buddy, who it turned out was blaming me for wrong information in their sample that he had provided me. Who better to throw under the bus to his boss, and probably to the global prospect as well, but me. He was literally screaming at me. Meanwhile the gate agent called our group. I politely and repeatedly told him I had to go, we were boarding. He just kept yelling over me. It ended with me politely apologizing that I had to go and hanging up. I was fuming as we boarded and Roger tried to talk me off the ledge. We landed in our seats and could finally breathe, both taking a deep sigh. At this point I asked: "Babe, what time is it?"

Roger usually threw his arm out a bit dramatically to reveal his Rolex; it was a quick move that I teased him about often. A bit reminiscent of an Inspector Gadget move, this approach to determine the time always gave me pleasure. So, "Babe, what time is it?" was followed by the classic wrist move only to reveal...no watch, a totally empty wrist. He immediately realized he did not have his money clip either. The money clip was a gift from me, custom made with his initials engraved on the back. Both of the watch and the money clip were very meaningful and both were still sitting in a bin at TSA.

Roger looked at me with sheer panic and said: "I am going back." I stood up with him and made a move to get my bag from the overhead. He said: "Stay here, I will be right back."

I sat in a panic, thinking what the hell am I going to do when he doesn't get back in time. I was sure he would not get back; he needed to deplane, run down an entire terminal, find the TSA lane we were in, see if they had the items, confirm they were his, run back, and reboard before they shut the gate. I was in a state of high anxiety, anticipating I would have to wrestle both our carry-on bags off the plane myself. I watched the door like a stalker, watching, watching, looking at the flight attendance, watching. Checking my phone. Waiting for any notice that I needed to yank our bags and go.

Instead, Roger came flying back onto the plane holding both items up like well-earned trophies from the Boston Marathon. He recounted that as he ran up to TSA, the agent recognized him and yelled: "Watch, money clip?"

"Yep that's me," Roger said, now proudly wearing his medals. I'll never know why he was even able to deplane and then reboard.

The National

IN 2015, AT THE BEGINNING OF MATEO'S SHOW CAREER, WE HAD A huge National show. As I mentioned, the National is a very big deal. Each year, every club for each breed (in our case SCOA, Spinone Club of America) hosts an annual event called the National. People come from across the US to attend and enter their dogs. For every breed's National show, there is a competition called conformation, which is essentially a show and judgement of how closely each dog adheres to the breed standard as documented by the American Kennel Club (AKC). There are also obedience competitions and, for Spinoni, hunt trials.

Going into the 2015 National, Mateo was the number one Spinone in the breed for conformation. He had already had an amazing show career from the time he started as a young dog. A fun element of the National is that often, at least one of the show's judges is from the breed's country of origin. This particular year, we had an Italian judge and a US judge, one for each day. Mateo had a professional handler, Carlos, one of the top in the country, who became a very close friend of ours over the years. He is a phenomenal human and connects with each dog in a way I have never seen. People take dogs to him from all over the country and even some from outside of the US. We were privileged to have him. He and Mateo had a beautiful bond and it was reflected in the show ring.

We had enormous respect for Carlos and his style was similar to ours, hardworking and a perfectionist. He worked insane hours and everything he did mattered to him.

On a standard show weekend, a big handler will typically show 12 to 20 dogs of different breeds for different clients. Nationals are difficult for all handlers because it is a week when they are only able to show for one client.

Carlos and Mateo showed beautifully at the 2015 National; it was beyond amazing to watch. Roger had stayed home with our other dogs. The show was not too far away from our house, a little over two-and-a-half hours away. At the first show, Mateo was awarded Best of Opposite. To simplify for those unfamiliar with dog shows, this is essentially second place out of about 80 dogs. That in and of itself was exciting for us. To make it even sweeter, it was the Italian judge who gave him the award and who kept repeating in his heavy Italian accent: "He's beautiful. He flies, he flies!" Movement is important for conformation. He even wanted to videotape Mateo as a representative of the breed.

On the second day with the US judge, the Regional for the National show, Mateo won. Of 80 wonderful representatives of the breed, Mateo won the breed. Between shows, we competed in obedience, and he earned an obedience title with me on the other end of the leash and became a therapy dog.

Roger surprised me and drove more than five hours round trip to celebrate at the awards dinner with me. The conference facility was very nice for our purposes, but definitely not anything fancy. It was so sweet of him to do that, so romantic and loving. He knew the joy this brought me, and he wanted to be part of the experience with me. My friends were beyond impressed. One of our friends is an amazing photographer and I'm so happy I have a photo of the two of us at that celebratory dinner. The effort and love Roger showed was and is second to none.

Prius in Neutral

ON SOME OF OUR TRIPS TO JACKSON HOLE, WE MET ROGER'S CLOSE friend and fly-fishing guide Joe, in Wyoming. Joe came from Colorado, so he drove down, usually the day after we arrived. We typically met at the top of Teton pass the day of their fly fishing adventures. Joe was used to camping and staying at low amenity hotels and even the random AirBNB with other people — strangers — definitely not how we rolled. We did not stay at the same hotels. In the early years, we stayed at these beautiful rustic style cabins in downtown Jackson Hole. In later years, we stayed on the Idaho side at new resorts and hotels.

I would head straight to Diana's after dropping Roger off with Joe. One year, we met at the top of the pass. Crossing the pass can be time consuming; winding up and down the steep edged pass for miles. This is the only road, and the way all trucks and cars take. Every year there are reports of vehicles going over the edge, especially trucks. No one survives that fall. There is only one emergency pull-off and no cell service in the mountains until you get all the way down to Jackson Hole or all the way up into Idaho.

We met at the top of the pass; the guys took the rental car, and I took Joe's car to Diana's house later in the morning. We met really early in the morning, since they had a couple-hour drive further into Idaho to the angler shop. The top of the Teton pass is absolutely beautiful, especially at sunrise or sunset.

I rode with Roger, half asleep, before the day's coffee, to do the exchange. Joe had his newer Prius pumping music and ready to go. Gear in hand and the CD he had made for the trip, one of Roger's favorite elements of the ride to the anglers, Joe was ready to switch cars. Roger was jacked for the trip. Beautiful barley and wheat fields lined the roads for miles and miles on the way, with great tunes playing, getting them geared up for a day of catching trout.

I jumped in the Prius, music still going, and headed down the mountain back to Jackson Hole, a 30-mile drive with no stops. I planned to go back to the hotel, work out, get ready, and then head to Diana's. There are switch backs the entire way down the mountain. I was expecting a smooth ride, albeit a windy one. Less than half a mile from where the guys headed on their merry way, and I looked down at the dash to see the Prius was on *empty*. The line was all the way past E. No cell service, no pull off, no fuel. Panic. I immediately turned everything off in the car, not a sound but my breathing. I was wide awake now. I strategically released the break as much as I could, shifting smoothly from drive to neutral as often as possible, taking every turn and declining. My biggest fear was whatever drops of fuel remained in the tank would shift and shut off the engine. I had a major emergency. A sudden shutdown could mean losing control and going overboard; the edge is so tight even a small car won't fit and I was worried about the car locking up if it ran out of gas.

Diana had shared many stories and I knew all too well what could happen if I ran out of gas in the wrong spot. She was always so careful doing that drive. I was as careful as possible, too, watching the dash as I counted the miles sliding down the mountain. I said many prayers and asked for miracles from guides, angels, and family on the other side. They had me covered that day; I *rolled* into the gas station at the bottom of the mountain and the car ran out of fuel as it slid to the pump with the deepest sigh of relief. I was not completely done with this adventure though; this was my first experience with a Prius, and I couldn't find the gas cap release switch – adventure number 2!

The Golden Goose

I HAVE ALWAYS BEEN A HUGE ANIMAL LOVER. I'M DRAWN TO HEIR pure love and beauty. I love how you can just see into their souls. As a child, I had many pets: dogs, cats, and even cows. For part of my young life, we had a large rural farm. I'm sure my mother's passion for animals drew me to them. Her entire family was also passionate about animals, her youngest sister, Tammy, in particular. When I was around six years old, my aunt, who was young with no children and didn't know the rules of the road, brought me a kitten while I was recovering from chicken pox. This didn't go over that well at home. Of course, I fell in love with the kitten, but we could not keep it. We had an older cat who had health issues. The last thing she needed was some punk kitten harassing her. I'm sure my aunt kept the kitten. She had a job at a pet shop for a while and ended up with every dog, cat, bird, and reptile that became homeless or had an issue and could not be sold.

We grew up vegetarian. We had this large farm, more than 60 acres, but we were not meant to be cow farmers. The cows had names and became pets because my mom could not stand the thought of sending them to slaughter. I knew none of this until I was an adult, but I absorbed that love for all of life's creatures.

As a kid I was a member of countless animal nonprofits, virtually adopting and donating whatever I could. In high school, I constantly donated to animal organizations. As an adult, I continue to contribute to many animal causes. I was able to act as a board member for a local animal shelter and I am very active in the dog community. I'm drawn to the pure simple way of life of animals, how they live in each moment — living out of love, total unconditional love. I have almost rolled my SUV to avoid squirrels or rabbits. I go out of my way to take bugs outside and I have helped recover many neighbors' loose dogs over the years.

I've been blessed with multiple "heart" dogs, the ones that come along once in a blue moon if you're lucky. They teach you lessons and show you love in a connected way that only animals can. For those not familiar with a "heart" dog, they are essentially your doggy soul mate. To date, I have been blessed with two and I am forever thankful.

I take this stuff very seriously.

One beautiful summer day, Roger and I were playing golf with his son, Jeff, on one of our favorite courses — a pretty course with three 9-hole courses. The course was loaded with geese, very common for golf courses in the Midwest. Groundskeepers put out fake foxes, owls, and whatever other trick is supposed to fool the geese into leaving, but geese love the courses. I don't know if it's the fresh aeration, the bugs, the open space, or grass seed, but they're drawn to hanging out on a golf course. They generally stay in the shady areas under the large trees to the left and right of the fairways, unless they are on the move. And they're so used to people, they just meander from one side to the other with no sense of urgency, no call to spread their wings and fly.

At the twelfth tee, the guys teed off first. I was up next, and I hit a nice long drive. Just as I hit, the flock decided to cross the fairway. I immediately felt anxious, as if slow motion. My anything-but-slow-motion ball T-boned a poor goose square in the side. I saw him go down.

I'm not ashamed to say I teared up. I felt awful and kept saying "I killed it, I killed it, I killed it," but I was too scared to look again. I'm positive Roger and Jeff we're doing everything in their power not to laugh, knowing that would not be the best response. Game faces on, they kept saying: "No, you just stunned it, it's fine." On the next hole I finally looked, and did not see a man (or goose) down in the previous fairway. I was filled with relief. As my vibe shifted, the guys finally felt comfortable enough to laugh; they had been holding it back for almost an entire hole. Roger had played many rounds and never had that experience before. He laughed, trying to get out: "What are the chances?"

3 Dog Limit

SOMETIMES MY CONNECTION WITH PETS MAKES ME FEEL MORE IN line with their energy and vibration than humans. Dogs especially have always been drawn to me and me to them. The beautiful unconditional love from dogs is precious. Once you've had that connection you always want it in your life. Of course, with deep connection comes risk of heartbreak. Given a dog's life span, if you love dogs and have them in your life, heartbreak is a given.

I had my heart dog, Dante, when Roger and I met. He was eight weeks old when I got him. When Roger and I were dating, I ended up rescuing two Yorkies, as well. Well, actually three. I rescued yorkies with health issues. One sweet little soul, Nicholas, did not survive his liver shunt issues. I lost him at only one-and-a-half years old, despite surgery, a special diet, and medication. He and my yorkie girl Maddy (who had a liver shunt, as well, but was lucky and healed beautifully) were very close. Nicky was four pounds of love, and loved to cuddle. He slept right on my shoulder. When Nicky passed, I had to give Maddy a new Yorkie playmate, so I rescued Max.

Maddy was a baby, only a few months old, when I rescued her, two pounds of adorable totally girly girl. But a *boss*. Maddy instantly owned the men in her life, *i.e.*, the men in my life, Roger and Dante. Roger adored Maddy. Dante gave her everything and anything she wanted: his food, his dog toys, the dog beds — even the extra-large ones. The 70 pounds he had on her meant nothing; if she wanted it, she got it.

One night just before Roger and I were get engaged, I brought Maddy with me to his townhouse for the evening. It was late and I was getting ready to leave. Roger was at the top of the stairs where the bedrooms were, I was directly below at the front door. As he came down, he said: "Maddy, why don't you stay with me tonight." She immediately rolled over and played dead. We had no idea she knew how to do this; she had never done it before. We were crying laughing. Clearly she was going home with mom, but she and Roger adored each other. I eventually trained her to be a therapy dog. She was an ideal therapy dog and loved to sit next to a patient who would talk to her and love on her. In addition to therapy work with patients, Maddy got lots of lap time with dad, too.

When Roger and I moved in together and got married, I had three dogs. They were all easy keepers, except maybe Max. Male yorkies rarely get house trained. Nicky was potty trained, but it was a challenge with Max. He was a cute little guy with a bum leg, but man was he feisty. Good thing he had lost a bunch of his teeth or he would have gotten in even more trouble. I had a routine and was completely used to three dogs. Roger, who adored the dogs, said that two dogs would be our limit in the future.

When we lost Dante, I had a tough time. It was the first time in my life I dealt with depression. The house was so quiet. I missed my beautiful, big-heart dog. It was about a year later when we got Mateo from a litter of Dante's lines. Mateo went to the big show, Westminster, and many other dog shows, earning top spot in history for the breed (grand champion points are what dogs earn when they win at a show with other entries of the same breed) by the time he was only four years old. Roger frequently joked, as a former college athlete and scratch golfer, Mateo earned way more bling, ribbons, and rosettes than he ever did. He loved telling people about Mateo and the wins he had under his belt — I mean collar. I know part of it was because it brought me so much joy. Roger loved to bring me joy, so much so that he broke the two-dog rule he had implemented.

I introduced Roger to another awesome rare breed, the Dandie Dinmont terrier, a little dog with a big personality. Part of the long and low crew, Dandies are around 25 pounds and known for their big eyes and big noses. Their eyes look into your soul, something they have in common with their sporting dog cousins, the Spinone. I've heard, and it's been my experience, that Dandies are the least terrier of the terriers. Least terrier? What does that mean? Let's say a little less stubborn, a little less independent, a little less pigheaded, and they may actually listen occasionally.

Roger and I went with our handler Carlos to a local dog show to watch Mateo, who was rather early in his show career at the time. Carlos was showing a beautiful little Dandie girl named Angie from a client in California. I fell in love with Angie and I knew Roger would as well. Mateo loved all little dogs and, much to Angie's dismay, sat under her grooming table and cried to get her attention. Over the next year or so, the more we learned about the breed, the more we loved them. In 2016, a few months before my birthday, Roger gave me a huge surprise. He made arrangements with the top US breeder to get me a Dandie puppy. He told me ahead of time so I could have the joy of the journey: the pups being born, picking names, watching the babies grow, and months of anticipation and planning, all in preparation to bring our new addition home.

I was beyond surprised over a gift of such heartfelt and beautiful love. After the pups were born, we decided to get a male. I prefer boys as they tend to be a bit needier and more affectionate, which always draws me in. Happily violating the two-dog rule, we now had four dogs. We decided to name him Dallas (I'm a huge Dallas Cowboys fan, and Roger was a convert as well). The name is actually Scottish, which is the breed's origin, so it was ideal. His full AKC name was Starring the Big D, call name Dallas.

Dallas was instantly the biggest hit at our house. He knew his place with his new Yorkie siblings and perfected the art of active avoidance until he won them over. They were pretty tolerant and he knew his limits with both of them. Mateo was so excited to have baby Dallas in the house, he thought Roger had gotten *him* a puppy. Fair enough, as Mateo's birthday is a month after mine. Mateo now had a legit play buddy, since the Yorkies rarely "played."

Our trio had become the perfect golf foursome, thanks to my husband leading our home and my gifts completely with his heart.

Fair Game

BEFORE ROGER'S SON JEFF MOVED OUT OF STATE, THE THREE OF US frequently played golf on weekends, generally on one of three or four courses. Roger usually picked a current favorite and stuck with it until he had a new favorite, or rotated through a set of favorites. He always had multiple go-tos in the rotation. That philosophy went for many things, including food, restaurants, and vacations, as well as golf courses. If a certain thing fell off the favorites list, it could eventually come back into the rotation. Roger loved having a routine for the key elements of his life. One of our favorite local courses had a beautiful practice facility known as one of the best practice facilities in the Midwest. Just 30 minutes from home with two 18-hole courses and the practice facility, this course was always on our list.

Roger spent many hours at that practice facility. There was also a fully lit driving range, which made it perfect for any hour of the day. I have many videos of his gorgeous golf swing, taken at Saint Andrews or other courses, and even in our front yard. He hit many balls into the huge open field in front of our house. The videos all start with "ready?" from Roger, a mumbled yes from me, followed by his flawless swing; he may or may not have been happy with it, depending on the day. Many of these were shot early in the evening in front of the house, around dusk so he wouldn't get "busted" by one of our neighbors. We took them all times the year, and in most weather. That went for golf practice, hitting golf balls, putting (in the living room), or playing. I learned early on if the temperature was above 36 degrees, it was fair game to walk and play. In late fall or even full-on winter, I bundled up to play and we would walk the round.

One year, I got Roger a special set of irons for Christmas. They were the previous year's model and no longer in production. Roger was very particular about his equipment. He had even done advertisements for Wilson Golf back in the day when they owned the industry. According to Roger, the new model of the clubs he was playing were not as good; just not the same. They had changed the clubs and sunsetted the model from the year before, so finding a brand-new set — a requirement of Roger's — was almost impossible. The true players were all trying to get them, including two pros at one of the courses we played.

I found them brand new on eBay. I bet on them aggressively and got them just in time for Christmas. Come to find out, I was bidding against one of the said pros who was desperately trying to win them. Christmas usually falls well past golf season in Chicago, but this particular year, Christmas week happened to be in the 40s and we played golf on Christmas Day. I'm sure it was 40s because I don't recall being "toasty." We walked out on the course and got in the majority of 18 holes with Roger's new clubs in tow.

Shadow Work

LATE FALL OF 2017 WE EXPERIENCED OUR DARKEST HOURS AS couple and individually. The hours the business required didn't leaved us space, or we weren't finding space for us — for fun and the deep personal communication which we were both needed. This, coupled with insecurity, landed us in a foreign place. We were 24/7 work and it led to a huge misunderstanding. It was the holiday season and that meant even more stress. I take full ownership of my role in stepping back, stepping away; we split up for six weeks. It's hard to say we were split, however, as we didn't do that well at all. I think deep inside we both knew we were each other's home, and we wouldn't truly split. Even though I was technically the one who left, I felt the deepest loss, not knowing what was to come. I walked outside or on the treadmill and just cried all the time. We still had a great deal of connection, working together every day and talking constantly. I typically stopped by to see him about once a week as well.

I know my decisions at that time were driven by fear. I was so scared to lose Roger, to get my heart broken, I ended up breaking it myself. Our separation happened right before Thanksgiving, but before New Year's Day we were fully back together. I started seeing Roger again and having tough, deeply emotional conversations. We were both in so much pain not being a couple. On New Year's Day, I asked if I could see him. I offered the deepest, most meaningful, heartfelt apology I'd ever given. I remember the total joy we both felt after that conversation. He kept saying he had redemption, that this entire thing was inexplicable, but now he understood. I think we both had inadvertently triggered each other's deepest wounds, our inner child wounds. This beautiful conversation brought us to a place of healing. I never felt more bliss, more at peace, a deeper connection, and contentment in my heart and soul than when we got back together.

As much as I beat myself up over every single detail of the separation and regretted the pain, I know we were closer than ever afterward. I knew there was nowhere else for me. His heart and soul were with mine forever.

In many ways this experience was a foreshadowing. I already knew the pain of not physically having him, but the beauty was and is that I have him closer and deeper than ever. That experience made us create space for the two us. We took many trips, not for work, just for us. Even a weekend getaway wasn't just a weekend getaway, it was pure love and joy. We joked how we had it all, the fun, excitement, and butterflies of a couple's first blush of love, and the comfort and knowingness of our forever. We knew each other better than anyone knew either of us. I have so many gorgeous memories I come back to over and over from our 20 years together, and many specifically from that time. We blocked out so much outside noise and were in total union. We were totally present with each other and invested in us.

The experience made us even closer and stronger, and prepared us for navigating new communication systems and getting back to basics. We became completely heart centered, leaving fear and ego aside, because ego and fear weren't serving us as individuals or in our union. All of that is completely

Lindsay Stanton

stripped away with Roger now on the other side. Our union is pure light and love. We were and are here to serve together, to try and help others, to share our story in hope of providing hope from of our love and infinite bond.

Oxon Hill

SPRING OF 2018 WAS FILLED WITH HEAVY RAINSTORMS. ROGER AND I headed from Chicago to Maryland for a work conference. We were going to meet with several large client companies in the staffing and outsourcing industries, as well a few prospects. We had a few days of heavy meetings scheduled, then a quick turnaround the day after the event for more meetings in Chicago. I had the opportunity to speak at the event, which was beneficial for the company, great exposure, and validation of our position in the marketplace. We had become synonymous with the technology we provided that no one in the industry offered. In 2019, we secured a patent around the core of our technology, which gave us a first mover advantage we had worked hard to build and maintain.

The event was hosted at one of the coolest hotels and conference properties we had ever seen. It wasn't necessarily the fanciest, although it was very high end, but it was a super cool space. We had been many places around the world and been exposed to a lot of nice facilities with a wide variety of amenities. Here, our bathroom had lights that turned on and off via voice command, and it featured only sleep safe lighting — no blue light. The bathroom mirrors lit up in various ways and colors for doing makeup, and there was a mini-TV in the corner of the mirror. We could control music and the television, and even check the weather by voice. We were able to set the lights to turn on automatically when we entered. To top it off, we were surrounded by windows and there was a gorgeous view of the city at night.

One night, we went out to a nice dinner, just us. We took a selfie in the room before we left. I love that photo. The amazing room lighting helped, but the photo totally captures our essence — the balance of our masculine and feminine energy, the joy we have in each other, and our unlimited connection.

We always had the ability to navigate any challenge, not get stuck in it. Not dwell on one thing, but flow through the good, the bad, and the ugly. We never even saw challenges as challenges, that is how little we focused on them. We moved in multiple directions as a team with big goals and agendas and thrived.

After a few days of meetings, we headed to the airport to fly back to Chicago when a series of spring storms hit the East Coast and Midwest. Our flight was cancelled, but our assistant did an amazing job of getting us the last two seats on another flight.

We had to hustle; the rebook was an earlier flight than our original and on a different airline, which meant a different terminal. As runners, we could move when necessary. We ran from the car rental to check-in, got through security quickly with TSA pre-check and flew to the gate. Before first group started to board, the flight information changed to "delayed." It was delayed over and over; as every new boarding time got close, and they would move it back again. This went on for hours. By late evening we decided to grab dinner close to the gate. The man next to us was from Baltimore and told us that this happened when there are storms, and once it hit 9:00 p.m., there was a ninety percent likelihood they would cancel the flight entirely. As we finished dinner, we knew what was in store next. We had to get back to Chicago for our meeting the next day. We ran to the rental car area, worried others may have the same idea, got a car, and hit the very stormy road. In ideal conditions, it would have been about an 11-hour drive. This spring night there were countless hours of complete white-knuckle driving between Baltimore and Chicago. I am forever thankful for Roger owning most of the driving that night in such stressful conditions. We still managed to have fun, with amazing conversation and awesome music fully on tap.

In the early morning hours we stopped at McDonald's — the only place open — to grab coffee. We needed a caffeine fix and break from windshield time. In full Mickey D fashion, they were promoting some movie, probably Disney and definitely a cartoon, and the main character from it. They had these huge masks with big teeth that you hold over your face and it looked like half your face was the Joker's grin. We could not stop laughing and messing with it over our lattes.

We rolled into Chicago just in time to shower, grab more coffee, and head to our meeting. Considering the experience, we were energized. The company representatives we met were shocked we were even upright, let alone functional. We were a true team that day, as we have been a true team since we met. We have been a team in many lifetimes and, as a team, we navigate this new challenge of physical separation.

Berlin

I AM A HOMEBODY AT MY CORE, AS WAS ROGER, SINCE THAT IS where we both felt most comfortable. We always welcomed the quite ease of our time just us at home. There was a peace and truth to us when we are alone. We were "at home" when we were together, which allowed us to travel more than either of us probably would have if not for each other. That has been one of the biggest challenges for me. Roger was where I felt most at home. With the transition to the non-physical, a large part of my work has been learning and reminding myself that now we are always together. We don't have the restraints of the physical. We were each other's home, we are each other's home, at the soul level. We knew this the minute we met. He verbalized it and wrote it; he memorialized the acknowledgement of his soul's recognition.

At the peak of my work schedule, I was doing multiple trips a week, sometimes not going home in between. Luckily, Roger and I were together eighty percent of the time. I don't get nervous travelling and never did when we were physically together. It has never been nerves about travel, it's more a longing to be home, to be in my routine, where I/we are most comfortable.

International travel is not really my thing. Spending eight hours or more sitting on a plane is a major challenge for me.

We both struggled with this. Fortunately, neither of us slept on flights, so we could just relax and talk.

In 2018, we headed to Berlin. It was my first trip to Germany and Roger hadn't been in more than 20 years. I had a speaking engagement at a large global conference. Roger was helping me with meetings we had set up, including with a new global partner that hosted the event. We had plenty of meetings on the books with several CEOs and executives, including our partner.

I was skeptical of what I was going to eat on this particular trip. I'm mostly vegetarian, but occasionally eat fish. Roger was a particularly picky eater with a relatively short list of items that made his cut of "consumable." Neither of us ate rich, heavy, or fried foods. We stayed at the Westin in the government district, close to all the foreign embassies, a beautiful area. Berlin is a gorgeous city with amazing architecture; there is so much richness in the streets, buildings, and shops. One evening we walked the shopping part of the city, hitting iconic stores like Gucci — such a unique experience.

We ate dinner at our hotel one night, but while walking around another evening, we found this hole-in-the-wall Italian place, very tiny with a small outdoor eating area. Roger had been really hot in the conference venue with a dress shirt and jacket on; it was close to 80° during the day and there was no AC, so the evening temperatures were ideal. We had just left the conference, and it was early still; we were super messed up with the change in time zones and jet lag. It was early for dinner, but the place was already busy with patrons eating there and taking meals home. Many of the locals knew this place and those who worked in the district made sure to get there early — all promising signs for a tourist. The weather was perfect, unseasonably warm for October. We sat at a cute little tabletop out front. One of the owners of this little restaurant and all the staff were from Italy and befriended us.

We ordered off the menu the first night and made fast friends with the staff. At one point, Roger invited one of the owners to sit and chat with us, which he willingly did. It was one of the best meals we'd had anywhere, so of course, we went back. It was definitely a top ten on our list of dinners: excellent food, romantic setting, and wonderful company, including fun, friendly owners.

The second night we were both prepared to reorder the exact same thing we ordered the night before. Why mess with a good thing? We did reorder the same appetizer, but the owner leaned in and whispered to us they had just made a special truffle pasta for themselves only. They were not offering it to patrons. A creamy truffle sauce peppered with pine nuts, a light amount of glazing and shredded cheese was served over a stuffed pasta with some type of amazing mushroom I had never experienced before or since. The dish was garnished with grape tomatoes sliced around the edges of the plate. The result was perfection. Roger was nervous to go to this level of exploration, but he recognized the opportunity and the respect of being offered this special item by the owner, so he could not say no. He was completely unsure of the description. He wasn't a mushroom person and never ordered a cream sauce. I rarely do either, so this was a complete exercise in trust. The result: he all but licked his plate in amazement. We had made new friends in a new city with an amazing romantic culinary experience to boot.

Interlude

YOU PROTECT ME WITH YOUR SHIELD OF UNCONDITIONAL LOVE. YOU created a safety, a loving, a knowing, deep within me. I feel it truer and stronger than I ever have in this lifetime. It is as if what was a pond became an ocean with the strength of the shore of your love.

Green Lake

ONE OF MY FAVORITE PLACES AND TIMES THAT WE SPENT TOGETHER was at Green Lake, Wisconsin. Neither of us had known of this pristine spot until 2018. Right after the new year, we decided to do a romantic winter weekend. We stayed at the Heidel House resort right on Green Lake. This hidden gem, absolutely quiet and beautiful, is only a few hours from Chicago, the perfect length drive to enjoy great tunes and great conversation. The cute little town, with its small restaurants, was exactly the downshift and alone time the two of us needed. The resort felt very private. It was the ultimate mini vacation for us: no outside noise from work, friends, or family. Pure us, back to the beginning of our soul connection. It felt like a beautiful and familiar restart. I'd take myself back to this trip, and others that followed to Green Lake, frequently during my visualization practices several years later.

The first late January trip was particularly wonderful, with the snow lightly frosting the lake and the overlooking trees. We learned the places to go and secret language of Green Lake. We were in love with this new-found town, our perfect little getaway, so I tucked this one into my brain for future reference.

I am and always have been very selective about the gifts I give for birthdays, holidays, and celebrations. I love giving gifts that are meaningful to those I love most. The time and effort of planning is how I show how much I love them; this is what matters most to me. I have never felt stronger about this than with Roger. When spring rolled around that year, I started planning for my Gemini hubby's birthday.

Roger was obsessed with golf. It was everywhere in our home: on television—the golf channel, even taking practice swings in the living room or practice shots on the front lawn, which often included filming for post-swing review. If it wasn't golf on TV, it was the news or The Weather Channel in preparation for golf. Roger was the family meteorologist, always knowing upcoming weather patterns after a lifetime of playing golf. He had played since he was seven and earned a full-ride scholarship in college. He had every opportunity and reason to be passionate for the game.

Roger had the privilege of playing just about every famous golf course, including Augusta multiple times. He took me to play gorgeous courses, including Torrey Pines in California. Golf and fly fishing where his twin passions and allowed him to be his most pure self, in nature, enjoying every minute of the bond with the earth and the sport.

When I discovered Lawsonia Links golf course in Green Lake, the perfect gift was brewing. Lawsonia is a stunning historical venue built in the 1920s and '30s, with two 18-hole courses. The courses have a throwback feel, as if they were in Scotland or Ireland, not central Wisconsin. We played the Woodlands course the first day and the Links course the second day, and they both lived up to their top 100 reputation. The gorgeous greenery of these golf courses was as beautiful as the lush forests we'd hiked over the years, every hill and undulation full of glory. The courses were long but playable for me, and Roger thought they were a dream, accommodating his refined skillset perfectly.

We started the weekend with a great Wisconsin Friday night fish fry. Probably the best we had ever had, and ended with a drive home talking about the stunning, nostalgic golf course. In addition to visualizing us at the golf course with its large greens and lush foliage, I have a little video that makes my heart smile; I end up laughing every time I watch it.

I had called the resort ahead of our trip and told them it was Roger's birthday. They set the room up with cute balloons and a little gift card for two free drinks at their bar. Attached to the balloons with a ribbon was a small mesh gift bag that included various mini chocolate bars — Hershey's, Mr. Goodbar, dark special, and a peanut butter cup. We joked that the best thing in the little bag was the peanut butter cup. When Roger was in the other section of the suite, I carefully untied the bow, stole the peanut butter cup, and put everything back so it looked untouched. The next day after golf, we were both very hungry. He walked up to the balloons, while I was discreetly filming on my phone, and unwrapped the treats, immediately realizing I had stolen the peanut butter cup. He gave me the cheekiest grin. I think he enjoyed that trick as much as I did. We both got such a laugh, and I am so thankful for that moment, that video, that trip, and that amazing, beautiful man.

Charleston

WE TOOK SO MANY BEAUTIFUL TRIPS OVER THE YEARS THAT PICKING a favorite is impossible. Even narrowing down the top five is challenging, but Charleston was one for the record books. Neither of us had been to Charleston. On paper, it seemed like a perfect spot for us. The style of dress, the unique historical hotels, the shops, and don't even get me started on the restaurants — the food was amazing. When I was planning the trip, narrowing down a short list from so many five-star restaurants was difficult.

Our Charleston trip was over the 2019 New Year. The trip was a surprise, my Christmas present to Roger. By fate or happenstance, we both got each other a trip as gifts for Christmas that year. Roger loved to know what was coming, so a trip at Christmas for New Year's, leaving in only a few days, was a risk. But I knew he was drawn to Charleston and I had a trump card — a round of supreme golf.

Roger always dressed impeccably. In high school and college, he had worked for the top men's clothing store in Des Moines, Iowa. He loved classic men's style with a hint of southern flavor. Some of his favorite stores, designers, and shoe manufacturers were based in Charleston. He was a classic center vent guy, and loved a traditional cut in a sport coat or a suit. He wore them so well. With heavy broad shoulders and a slender build, he was a suit's dream. And with his gorgeous bone structure and cheekbones, he looked like he stepped out of an ad for any high-end men's clothing brand.

I had the entire trip planned out. I had managed to get us a round of golf at The Ocean Course on beautiful Kiawah Island. With five separate 18-hole golf courses and endless views, the area is breathtaking. The Ocean Course is walking only and the entire course is on the ocean. Walking lets you take in every gorgeous inch of it. On many holes, you could walk out into the ocean from the fairway. In the morning, a thick fog lifts over the ocean and the course. The grounds are impeccable, one reason they held the 1991 Ryder Cup and the 2021 PGA Championship there. The Ocean Course is known for its difficulty impacted by the holes and course length, as well as the wind, which can really rock. The average wind is 10-20 mph, and that does not include gusts coming off the ocean. Roger loved playing in wind. I think it started in his childhood golf days and continued as he played college golf. The Ocean Course is a beautifully styled and designed course, and Roger loved the great Pete Dye layout. With the wind we were all set, but were warned not to go looking too hard for a ball... one of the nine-foot crocodiles may have found it first.

We were paired with a fit and friendly younger couple who had never played the course either. We enjoyed every minute of the course's difficulty, as well as the gorgeous practice area, clubhouse, and homes surrounding it. On the drive in that morning, beautiful houses to our right were all raised on huge pillars in preparation for the next storm. These same southern mansions lined the tee boxes and fairways throughout the course.

Our first night, we ate at this amazing Italian restaurant off the beaten path in the Park Circle area of northern Charleston, quite a ways from where we were staying downtown. I'm pretty confident there were question marks popping up in Roger's mind about my choice. The restaurant was in a bar district, and when we first walked in it gave a Tavern-type vibe. Roger's concerns were quickly squelched when the appetizers arrived. He talked about that meal for years, and he was such a picky eater. We started with a Pomodoro and mozzarella appetizer, which he inhaled — very rare for Roger. I seem to remember his dinner was spaghetti and meatballs — he was all about the classics.

We played a local public course on the trip as well. No great shakes, as Roger would say, but it allowed us to get a round in on New Year's Eve Day. We had big plans that night, so sneaking in a quick public round was perfect and, even though it was a smaller course, there were still plenty of crocs.

We had not eaten all day, but had dinner reservations at a great seafood place before the gala we had planned, so we wanted to grab something quick and not too big to hold us over. I went on Yelp to see what I could find, something walkable so we didn't have to spend time waiting for the valet to get our car. I found this five-out-of-five-star place less than half a mile from our hotel. Perfect. We were staying a stone's throw from the college campus, and as we walked along we got deeper and deeper into college housing territory, with plenty of Greek houses in the mix. We got to a laundromat when GPS announced "you've arrived." We thought *No, we haven't*. To our left was a coffee shop that may or may not have served more than coffee. We walked into the laundromat to ask and all around us were washing machines and dryers— total laundromat — except for the high top stools and counter at the back right by the windows tucked behind the entrance. It was a small counter, with a large chalkboard listing the most innovative grilled cheese sandwiches and classic milkshakes I've ever seen.

Major hesitation was oozing out of Roger and even me. But we'd come this far, and what was the risk factor of a grilled cheese sandwich? That was the best fucking grilled cheese sandwich ever, and I even took a few hits off of Roger's milkshake — also a win. A perfect meal that hit the spot before getting fancy for a big New Year's Eve night out.

Roger always let everyone know, including me, that he was proud to be with me. He made me feel so special. I'm not sure why he felt I was so worthy, but it was the most warmth, love, and acceptance I've ever felt. I loved to dress for Roger, and the dress I bought for that evening ended up being one of my favorite dresses of all time: a black formal to the floor, very fitted, with flecks of cut through lace throughout. A beautiful BCBG gown, it was anything but a basic black dress. I got so many compliments on it that night,

We were in the mirrored elevator heading down to get our car — mirrors all around us. Without giving me notice, Roger snapped a photo of me standing in the corner of the elevator. The mirrors caught his reflection, smiling at me in that dress, with the cutest Cheshire cat grin. Pure love, pure adoration, so much joy. It was a perfect New Year's spent with the perfect person, my soulmate, I want to ring in any and every celebration with him.

Letters

LOOKING BACK ON ROGER'S GORGEOUSLY WRITTEN LETTERS BRINGS up so much emotion, letting my love and grief collectively take center stage. Reading them now fully represents their truth, the deep knowing he expressed that I never would have predicted.

Though we met when he was being hit with so much loss from different angles, different layers, that there was no way for him to fully process it, at his core he knew love was all that mattered. At the end of each of our days, all that matters is how we showed up and how we loved. How we love ourselves and how we represented our love to our family, our friends, and everyone we encountered. How we impact the universe with our love and gifts.

Roger's letters gave me so many gifts. For years, he occasionally gave me a full letter or heart felt note, pouring out his truth, his love. No Fear, no need to protect himself in any sense of falseness — just one hundred percent his truth. Within the first hour of us meeting, he told me he would fall in love with me. He doubled down and represented that authentically and frequently in the early days and throughout the years of our journey.

Now when I look at the words he wrote, every letter speaks of how he knew immediately when we met that I was the girl of his dreams. In his spoken words and in each letter, he said that I was the girl he had imagined as a little boy, the girl he had dreamed of and pictured in his mind. His girl! He had envisioned *us* all those years ago as a child. Reading this, in the eloquent way Roger communicated, there was an immediate and deep knowing, a recognition back in time. The power of his feelings, the intensity of his connection with me was a soul recognition. He was so advanced at a soul level; he recognized the connection we had as soon as I walked through that warehouse door. We had known each other before. I look back on those early days and reflect on the language in his letters and recognize the universe truly did indeed come together and conspire to bring us together. Roger even said in one of his letters he felt we were drawn together intentionally.

I know we were. Many of his letters reflect on my love and compassion for others and how I helped him during his darkest hours. As I now face biggest, most tragic loss I could have ever been dealt, I look back at this time in his life, at the love and grace with which Roger led when most would hide in a corner, withdraw into themselves, protecting fiercely what little bits they felt they had left. Not Roger. Roger opened himself up fully to experience it all, to experience love and light. I was not fully aware at the time how our love impacted his healing. We were so inseparable and totally focused on us. Reflecting back, I can now appreciate at a deeper level all he handled. He spoke in his letters of my beauty and gifts, of my femininity, which was a reflection of his desire to experience my love and warmth.

We often sat up and talked all night. When Roger became sick and made the decision to go into hospice care at home, we returned to our roots. Our soul level connection is forever.

We knew that first day we met, and he was intuitive enough to memorialize it in writing for us. The last few weeks he was here physically, we talked all night long. We shared random stories and conversations, and spoke of our reunion and our future. The love and deep roots that drew us closer and closer in our early days were with us strongly again.

One afternoon, about a month before Roger passed physically, I was driving, deep in thought. I believe a divine knowing came over me, what some refer to as a divine download. I was never sad when we were together, that was very important to me. I never thought of being alone or losing him. I am very thankful I was able to stay present. I didn't really experience pre-grief. Of course I had times when I totally lost it, but not while we were together. Together time was sacred and I wanted every second of it. During a drive like this, I might normally start to cry, but not on this day. This day I had a calm wash over me and this thought that I am sure was not actually mine, but that came from somewhere much higher: a higher source, my higher self, a divine source, or angel. The thought was a deep knowing that this was not the end, not how we end, not the end but just the beginning.

As soon as I got to Roger, I told him my experience and he also had the same deep knowing. We knew this was just a transition period, that his physical body was not capable of housing all his gifts any longer. He needed to transition out of it, but that was okay, because this was just the beginning. This conversation was the foundation of many conversations between us that I deeply believe helped open the pathway of our communication once he was on the other side. We set our intentions during those last 30 days and every day I know we continue to live them. I have the opportunity to represent *us* physically. He has the opportunity to help guide me and use the amazing insight and access he's gained being on the other side. This is just the start of our journey — we have just begun.

Signs

THE NUMBER ONE TOOL TO HELP OPEN YOURSELF UP TO THE OTHER side is meditation. I have found meditating before bed extremely helpful. Meditation helps open my mind to receive messages from my loved ones on the other side and the divine in general. I initially started meditating before bed just to assist with my sleep. Even pre-grief, I always struggled with sleep. Being high drive, I could never stop thinking, I never was good at shutting off my head. I am a very light sleeper too, so the smallest noise, dimmest light, or even just sensing someone new in the room would wake me. With grief, I have found myself needing much more sleep. Even though I was exhausted, prior to starting a meditation practice that didn't translate to deep sleep. Meditation allowed me to get the deepest sleep I've ever had.

What does that mean for you? Meditation and deep sleep are often a pathway to receive messaging. You don't need to have a long-drawn-out meditation either. I have a set nighttime routine that helps me open up and puts me in a clear state to receive. The entire process takes only about 15 minutes and can be shorted to five minutes if necessary.

First, I generally do a very short walk around the block to help clear my head from the day. Then I do a three-minute chanting meditation. I have found the chanting meditation to be extremely helpful for a variety of reasons. The chanting mediation I specifically use is from Jay Shetty's book *Think like a Monk* At the end of the audible book's meditation chapter, Shetty offers three minutes of chanting mantras that are very soothing and open the flow. I generally start with this and then follow the chants with a five-minute visualization meditation. If I'm running low on time, I just do the three-minute chanting meditation.

For those who think they can't meditate, I highly recommend the short chanting meditation. It's impossible to think distracting thoughts and chant a mantra at the same time, so it's a great starting point. For visualization, I have three places that I primarily I take myself. They are particularly beautiful, joyful memories of Roger and I. While I tend to visualize just a few places, I often picture different actions, elements, conversations, or even music. I put myself completely there and genuinely feel it is current day. I view it as an opportunity for Roger and I to meet in another realm. This visualization realm offers us an opportunity to be together. I have a deep knowing that these activities and routines help facilitate the ability for us to connect at night. I journal almost all of my signs, angel numbers, other special gifts (we have established symbols and animals that we use to communicate), as well as my dream visitations. This is something I have done from the very start.

I journaled all our important, beautiful, long conversations before Roger transitioned to the other side, so it felt natural to me to journal signs and messages right away. I have a special journal just for us and keep it close at hand at night. I frequently get up in the middle of the night and write about our visits. I found our visits typically come between the hours of 2:00 and 4:30 a.m., and it's not uncommon for me to come out of one just in time for an angel number. I go into the bathroom for some light by which to write and frequently see 2:22 or

4:44 on the clock as I grab my journal. You are most open to receive while in your deepest sleep. I have found it is very important to write everything down as soon as you come out of the dream visitation. Writing detailed bullet points or even shorthand can help trigger the full experience and memory, so you don't forget elements when you fall back asleep.

I have even had two visitations in the same night. It is such a blessing when this happens, and they are generally back-to-back. Sometimes the first visit experience correlates with the second and sometimes they are completely separate experiences. Documenting details is important. As when loved ones communicate through mediums, sometimes when they communicate within a dream visit, they use symbols or information you may need to digest in order to fully understand the message. You may need to let the message sink in to understand any to-do items you have been given.

We established a fast and effective way of communicating pretty quickly, and Roger sends messages my way for others, especially family. This is even more reason to journal, because you may not be able to fully assemble the pieces until you speak with the family member involved. The message may relate to something they are experiencing, their grief, feelings of guilt, or even a song they have been listening to thinking of their loved one.

Trust is so important, fully understanding and trusting in the process. At the end of the day, what you do have to lose? Nothing to lose and absolutely everything to gain. You truly have the opportunity to have a complete and gorgeous relationship with your loved one. They are just no longer restricted to the physical body. For anyone skeptical, let yourself fully trust. Open yourself purely and watch what unfolds. The experiences will forever change the way you view the world and the purpose of our transition.

Another very important note on this topic of signs and messages is the more you receive, the more you will receive. There comes a bit of a tipping point when you are fully trusting and invested in your communication. You've blocked out negative outside noise and kept yourself grounded, knowing what you are experiencing is true. You have fully tapped into your soul's deep knowing. You start to remember at a soul level and this new trust and openness takes you to what I refer to as "next level signs," where they are just constant; there is a beautiful build, like a musical crescendo. It builds and builds, and the frequency increases, as well as some of the intensity. When I say intensity, I mean feelings you experience deeply, emotionally, viscerally. You may experience many lighter signs throughout a day, a few days, or even a week or a month and then — bam — a huge one. When you trust and let go into it completely, it becomes this amazing gift of ebb and flow.

One thing I had to do was to give up on the what, how, and when; give up what I thought it *had* to look like.

Some signs change. For instance, I had a very strong sign reoccurring over and over again for more than a month. It was a very specific sign and always happened at a purposeful time or during certain thoughts I had throughout my day. Then one day that sign stopped; but before it stopped completely it stopped at the normal time, popped up and stopped. This happened a few times, like a heads up for the winding down of this sign. I got nervous and was crying one day, talking to Roger, asking him why, what happened, what did I do, did I do something different, something wrong? Did I inadvertently do something to shut down our communication? Or at least block him from sending that specific sign? After that a few minutes of me saying these things in my head and crying, he sent me that sign, but then within an hour he sent me a different sign and I made the connection. I asked him the question and felt revalidated that we were just not doing that one specific sign anymore, at least for now.

The signs are so exciting, it is easy to get into a pattern of gluttony. I found myself really feeling my grief if I hadn't seen a sign or if maybe I'd missed one. I got paranoid. I worried I had done something to shift or stop the communication, or that I had started doing something that was blocking me. But I figured it out over time, with trust and a bit of trial and error. I was always connected, I just needed to learn a huge lesson: just trust. Of course, our transitioned loved ones want to be helping us, loving us, and showing us warmth; but even though they are not restricted in time or space like we are in the physical world, they have learning and responsibilities on the other side.

I know I have said the word trust often in this section, but it's a game changer. Just trust.

Let It Go

"LET IS GO" IS A PHRASE WE HEAR OFTEN WHEN DOING SPIRITUAL work, "self help," meditation, manifesting, and most things related to healing. This term just does not feel good to me. I have shut off books, podcast, and stories just because they started talking about "letting it go." Early on, I felt the push back from this phrase deeply. I didn't *want* to let it go. I wanted to hold on more than ever, to hold on to the pieces more than I have ever wanted or needed anything. I wanted to hold on to our memories, hold on to our love, hold on to our connection, hold on to our life/lives, hold on to our joy, hold on to our friendship, and hold on to every fiber of connection that meant the world to me.

So, for me the term "let it go" did not resonate. When I listened to affirmation mantras or even helpful books, I tuned out the parts that related to letting go. Those of us who have experienced loss, who are navigating traumatic grief, struggle with this saying. When in the throes of deep grief, it does not work to let it go. I was surprised how often this expression is used and I found often it is used without setting context.

As I have moved through this journey, I have reframed the phrase "let it go." Anytime I hear it now, I shift the view to one that resonates. For me now, let it go only refers to the *how*. It does not mean the what and certainly not the who. I am not letting us go — any part of us — past, present, or future. I am only releasing what I formerly knew as the *how*: how we were, the how that made us, the how we would be together. I released and gave in to a total lack of knowing how we experience our love and our bond without the physical. Letting go of what I thought our future looked like before Roger transitioned. Letting go of the set vision we once established for our future. Letting go of needing to experience the same experiences we had on the physical plane. Letting go of the house we lived in together, the car we rode in, letting go of the vacations we took each year, letting go of the *way* we assisted each other in business. Letting go of these elements, letting go in this context actually did the opposite of creating fear in me over letting go. Releasing these limited views of the "how" opened the door wider, allowing that letting go to be a pathway to gorgeous, limitless, magical possibilities.

It meant letting go of my once very limiting view of life. It meant understanding the truly endless possibilities. Instead of putting everything in a neat little box, it was opening the box fully to let the light in and out. It was blowing the doors off the box.

Only when you have opened yourself to these endless possibilities, can you really and truly start to receive all the magic in store. The more you see how this shift serves you, the more you can trust and open further and further. It is, without a doubt, a process — an ever changing, flowing process. Everyone says to take care of yourself, to do self-care, be kind to yourself when you're grieving. You also need to give yourself space. Give yourself space to grow, to shift, to reprioritize, to tap in, to express emotion. In my experience, you vacillate. You may think you have transitioned through one element just to be taken back there a few months later. Let that be okay. Feeling the feels is just as important as helping yourself manage the process. It is so important to let yourself have the cry, the melt down, the scream, the laugh. Allowing yourself to move into the emotion lets it move through you. Allowing the feeling means you won't get stuck. If you suppress it, it will find a way out eventually, likely in a less healthy way. Letting the feeling come over you and through you allows it to be in more of a wave. This ebb and flow helps you transition the grief. It also allows you to experience potential joy, as you start to transition the sadness by allowing in the memories of beautiful times you shared, or how your person would be right now in the moment with you. Would they be laughing at you, shaking their head, holding your hand? Be present and let your emotions ride the healthy waves they need to flow through you to experience the calmer ocean on the other side.

Let it go can be a safe space. Let it go can allow you to shift into a more open state. Let it go can allow you to receive in divine timing, in divine ways. Let it go means dropping your previous perspective and seeing the beauty in the open flow of the universe, our spirit team, and our loved ones on the other side.

SECTION 2

THE STORIES OF OUR LIFE IN THE PHYSICAL WORLD HELP PROVIDE the context of our relationship and the signs I have received daily since Roger's transition to the other side. There are so many forms signs can take. I have learned the art of the possible and not to let my mind limit what is possible. My initial belief, for example, that signs would only come in certain ways or forms, was limiting. I have learned that some signs are a pathway, they help create trust, they help you know you can communicate, and ultimately they help build your system of language. You are no longer limited to the audible or written language of communication. You are able to communicate through limitless methods. You just have to tune in to your perception to hear them.

I will share some of the ways we communicate to help you facilitate ways that will work for you. Be open, not only to receiving in the ways I mention, but to looking for others, as well. Be open to them shifting and changing over time. Don't be afraid when they do. I wish someone had told me that. Whenever I experienced a shift, part of me knew what was occurring, but part of me, my egoic mind, got bogged down in fear. I worried about the communication ending. Roger is my most important soul connection, and I worried about losing that. I did not know whether there was a process or time limit to when our loved ones on the other side could no longer communicate with us. I know now this does not happen. Roger has assured me, along with my guides, that they are not in a "phase" or "trapped" or anything like that. They can stay in communication with us and have their existence on the other side. Through constant communication, trust, love, and gratitude, I now completely know and live in the faith and complete confidence that Roger is with me every single day.

I also had a very deep intuition that Roger hears my thoughts and this has been proven thousands of times. I can communicate with Roger through my thoughts, through spoken word, and through setting my intention. I can also visit or call on him in more of a physical sense through visualization, which I will cover more deeply later in this section.

I talk to Roger all day, every day. Sometimes I tell him stories, ask what's happening on the other side, or ask him to help me with next steps in certain situations. Sometimes I ask him to provide insights or assistance. I often speak to him in my thoughts. At night, the last thing I do before I fall asleep is express my enormous gratitude for our soul connection to the universe, for continuing to open our pathway of communication; then I invite him in to visit me. I thank the universe and source for the amazing blessings and the beautiful relationship we have. I thank God, source, the divine for continuing to draw us closer. I announce my trust in the process and thank the universe for the outcome.

These statements of thanks and prayers of sorts help reinforce my connection and build confidence in our ability to connect. They facilitate our union and allow me to recap the blessings that I and we have created. They help us manifest our future; they enable a strong gateway to further manifestations.

Roger and I have built a truly amazing communication system for which I am overwhelmingly thankful. Our collective investments in building this system and me doing the work here on earth to facilitate the connection further, have provided the foundation we needed to create something truly magical. My goal is to help provide you the tools to do the same. *Our* goal is to show you the infinite possibilities through a few simple ways of cracking the door open to let in the light. Once you start to see what you can do, what your relationship is capable of, you will forever change the way you view a loved one passing.

I no longer use the words "death" or "die." We only transition. We transition from a physical existence that is no longer serving us. We are only less restricted. We did not lose; in many ways we gain. It is hard not having our person physically to hug, hold, be intimate with, or touch, but there is so much more. Now we can be with each other always, in all places at all times. It can serve as a freedom for us as well as those we love. If we can open our minds and hearts, we can see a pathway of so many beautiful possibilities, so many new ways to show and receive love. There are stunning miracles all around, just waiting for us.

Dream Visitations

DREAM VISITATIONS CAN TAKE MANY FORMS. I AM BLESSED BY THE amount and types of dream visits I have experienced since Roger's passing. Dream visits allow us to spend time with our loved ones in a more physical way. Dream visits are also a pathway for our loved ones to give us messages. These messages may be for us, or they may be for others. For example, Roger has sent me multiple messages during visits for his kids. He also, especially early on, provided insights on how to see him, how to receive signs and messages.

Our grief can block us from receiving messages; our family or friends may be limited in perception because of their deep grief. Your loved one's spirit will take the path of least resistance to communicate a message. You may be that path. When you are sleeping you are open and receptive. When you are trusted to share messages with others, that trust helps build your relationship and communication. Just as in the physical, when we share and deliver positive and powerful messages brought for others, our loved ones trust us and deliver more messages.

I wanted to share some of the types of dream visits I have experienced so you know some of what is possible. I am channeling parts of this book, and Roger has told me to tell you these are the ways we have experienced *so far*. The possibilities are endless.

When it comes to your dreams, I recommend journaling everything. This is very important, as details may be lost with time passing, and journaling is a beautiful tool to come back to if you're having a tough day or feeling ungrounded.

I really like journaling because I may need to digest the subtle messages of a dream visit or even talk it through with others, and journaling helps me track the details. I have found connections from a visit a day or a few days later, with messages I received being related to something going on in a family member's life.

You may find synchronicities with your visits and visits others have the same night. One night Roger visited me and a few days later I found out he had visited my dad the same night. There can be learning and messages in sharing your co-visits. Something that seemed small or minor to you may be important to a family member or connect to a challenge with their grief that you are meant to share. Journaling gives you the ability to fully absorb the visit and marinate on the details for more subtle messaging.

Simple Visits

THE FIRST TYPE OF DREAM VISIT I REFER TO AS SIMPLE VISITS. THAT is in no way meant to minimize their importance. Many times, they are very purposeful and happen just when we need them. One type of simple visit is a knowingness. You wake up and you know your loved one is or was with you that night. You know they visited, but there are no more details than that. When I have these kinds of visits, I wake up feeling so happy, so loved. I may even still feel or remember feeling an embrace. Roger and I were cuddlers at night and we generally cuddled in the spoon position. I might wake up feeling, or even partially knowing he was or is in that position with me. At the start of my journey, I tried to recall details of these visits and even got frustrated with myself that I could not pull up more of the specifics. Over time, as our communication has grown, I have learned to accept them for what they are and embrace the joy and comfort they bring. I see that it was an energy, an experience, and that it was what I needed — nothing more, nothing less. No need to stress over or fixate on the details. I view these visits like a hug you need after a tough day. That simple act of love can carry me through the day. The visits are a gift, such a beautiful reminder, an extra-special show of love from our person on the other side.

Message Visits

SOME VISITS ARE MORE PURPOSEFUL, MEANT TO SHOW YOU A specific message. These are more teaching visits. For example, I have been told during some visits that I have a purpose, a calling that I am meant to fulfill. Roger is helping me fulfill that purpose, telling me that we are a team, meant to help others, to show what is possible. His passing was to allow for this. We could not achieve this greater good, this purpose, if he had not transitioned when he did.

I have been told in message visits that my spirit animal is a Jaguar. I know this came from Roger and my spirit team because I had never given conscious thought to my spirit animal. I didn't know Jaguars could be spirit animals. After getting that message in a dream visit, I looked it up and was shocked that the description of a Jaguar as a spirit animal is completely who I am. Close family and friends agree the Jaguar spirit animal represents me perfectly.

Since that message, I have received many signs and validations where everything worked out and there was a Jaguar to thank for it. For example, I was in a major jam trying to get a ride to the airport in an area with no ride sharing, no available apps, no taxis, and it was a holiday where all private cars had been booked days before. Suddenly, I was presented with a business card for Jaguar Limo, who immediately picked me up.

Validation of these messages has shown up with my work as well. Messages have been woven into visits with Roger where he communicates something important that I likely would not have seen or done. For example, there have been times when I have done all I can in a challenging situation that is causing me stress, and Roger will show me all I have accomplished. He will frequently show the two of us (him by my side) doing the work. Then he will show me that all that could be done has been done and to let it go. In the dream, we will discuss or view the thing that's triggering me or stressing me out. He may show me the best way to handle the situation to achieve the highest outcome. In many cases, Roger and I are at work or in a place where I am experiencing a challenge. We may be in physical world discussing the issue and he shows me the way to handle it. Once I've seen the best option, I am able to release my need for control over the outcome, which is usually a huge stress reliever for me. It is so deep, the insight so powerful, that when I wake up, I can just let go and trust myself to handle the situation as I was shown in the visit. I did what I had the power to do, and now I have to trust. I could not have done these things without the insights from Roger's visits.

Downloads

THE OTHER WAY I RECEIVE MESSAGES IS THROUGH WHAT I CALL MINI downloads. It is as if the message is highlighted with the biggest highlighter pen in the universe. These tend to come overnight as well. They are unique and different from the other types of messages or visitations I receive. When they occur, I always have a space, quiet, with no message before or immediately after, so as to focus my concentration on what was presented. These messages tend to be short, one or two sentences, or even just a few words. Once I received a message that was silence, like someone hit the spacebar on a computer for 30 seconds, followed by the clear message: "God has a plan for you. You are here for a reason." This message came through loud and bold, and was followed by more silence, more space bar. These messages tend to occur during the same time frame, between 3:00 and 4:00 a.m.

Previews

PREVIEWS ARE ANOTHER WAY ROGER VISITS ME. PREVIEWS ARE AN opportunity for Roger to show me events before they happen in the physical world. There are a few types of events Roger previews for me in dream visits:

1. Significant event that he would have physically attended with me.
2. An event that may cause me stress or anxiety.
3. An event I am anxious about because I am physically going alone.

The perfect example occurred about a month after Roger's passing. Our company experienced a very stressful attempt at a hostile takeover by a few individuals. We went through an extensive process to get back control of the business. We called an emergency meeting with shareholders and I did a tremendous amount of work leading up to this meeting. The company was Roger's baby. We were both passionate about the business, and I knew how important it was to him, so I had to do everything I could to save it. A few nights before the emergency meeting, he visited and showed me what would happen in advance. During the dream visit, he and I were driving to the meeting in his car, talking on the way very positively and lovingly as partners. The atmosphere was completely calm. There was an ease when we walked into the meeting together. It was a hostile environment, but I said my piece calmly. Roger stood with me, but I was the only one talking. After the meeting while walking to the car, Roger said: "Now let it go, you've done what you can do. You must trust in the outcome, trust where the chips will fall." That dream visit was a total game changer for me. It allowed me to release all stress and anxiety around the outcome. This preview made me feel calm and confident going into the physical meeting, which ended in our favor.

Another example was at Roger's celebration of life. Due to COVID, we had to wait a year to have any type of memorial celebration. We scheduled it for the first anniversary of his passing, and I had a lot of anxiety leading into the celebration — anxiety about how people would bring up grief, how they would act, and what they would say, as well as the reminder of the physical loss. I was worried it would take me down a rabbit hole if there was conversation that didn't align with my experience or had a tone of finality or ending. I don't use the word death; it does not resonate with me at all. It was important to figure out ways to ground myself ahead of time to try and mitigate some of these feelings.

One thing that helps many of us when we are anxious about a new experience is to make it not be a new experience. When you have the comfort that you've been there or done that before, it significantly reduces anxiety. Roger took me through the celebration on two separate nights prior to the actual date in the physical world. Both times we were there, and he was by my side. People were talking and celebrating, and he was there with me, by my side. There was a knowing on my part that he was past his illness and totally well, that he loved hearing the kind words and experiencing the love he was being given. He loved the adoration and respect, and laughed at the funny stories and memories. I can't begin to express how much it meant to me to have this experience, how much it let me release my anxiety. It spared me so much stress and provided total comfort in the days and weeks leading up to the event. I was nervous on the drive to the venue, but that's all, which is pretty amazing given how traumatic it might have been.

Roger's daughter Meghan had to move the date of her wedding multiple times due to COVID. I would have likely had anxiety about not riding with Roger to the wedding, not getting ready together, not sitting together, not dancing together, and having to celebrate this beautiful day alone, without him physically with me. But those thoughts never came up. Roger helped me, showed me he would be there with me. Early on, I struggled to find a dress for the wedding and I had already ordered and returned many dresses. One night I said: "Babe, I'm sorry to bother you with this, but I want to represent *us* and I need your help with a dress." After that ask, at the very next store I visited, I was in the formal dress department and "Tainted Love" came on the radio. That song was absolutely a message. Roger and I always loved that song. It was pretty unfitting for the high-end department store, and it was such an old song. I walked in, heard the song, saw a beautiful metallic silver dress, and I knew — Roger drew it to me… for me. It was there just for me, for us.

I ordered butterfly earrings online for the wedding, gorgeous silver and diamond earrings to match the dress. Butterflies are one of Roger's signs to me — a very consistent sign. They arrived in a beautiful jewelry box tucked into a satin bag. When I opened the satin bag and took them out, a card fell out onto my dresser. The card included a small note that said: "Heart RJS!" Roger's initials. Total magic.

I received many consistent signs and messages leading up to an amazing preview visualization of the wedding, during which I was actually awake. I was walking on one of my favorite paths. I always feel especially connected and tuned in on this path. An Elton John song started to play on my phone out of nowhere. I had never heard the song before, it was a new remix. Roger and I were huge Elton John fans. That was the one of the last concerts we attended before he got sick. As I listened, I clearly saw Roger and myself at Meghan's wedding. At the time, I did not even know what the dance floor would look like, but I was shown every detail of it. Roger and I were on the dance floor, he in his tux, I in my silver dress — which I had not seen or bought yet — and we started dancing. Not just any dance. We started a complex, beautiful, choreographed dance. It was sensual, but also fun and cheeky — totally us. I could feel that everyone watching could see our love. I could feel our love with every fiber of my being. I was exactly where I was meant to be, in the arms of the person I was meant to be with. Our expressions and our attraction told our story — the total essence of who we are.

As soon as the song ended, the visualization was over. This gorgeous preview of the event was now a memory, and I can still see it in detail whenever that song plays. What an amazing gift Roger gave to me. We had our gorgeous dance at the wedding, our time, our celebration for Meghan with each other.

I hope the examples I have shared give you a good idea of what a preview can be. They are powerful experiences and such a blessing.

Physical Visits/Encounters

SOMETIMES THE HARDEST PART IS THE PHYSICAL LIMITATIONS OF our loved ones who have passed — our longing for that physical love and touch. I have found that visitations can fulfill that longing as well. One thing I miss most is kissing. I miss kissing Roger and being kissed by him, more than any other physical want or need. We solve that in dream visits, where we show each other love.

One night in particular, I was really missing his kiss and touch. During my pre-bed routine, when I always talk with him, I said: "Honey, I'd love to kiss you tonight. I miss kissing you." At that time, there was a lot going on with the business and many of our visits, though filled with warmth and love, had a lot to do with the company.

That night I had a visitation with Roger. We were at the office talking through some things I was dealing with in the physical world. I have found all my visits tie in with what's going on with me in the human world. We talked to some staff and were meeting with various team members in different areas of the office. When I headed back to my office, Roger followed, which happened often prior to his passing. When the conversation was over, he started to leave, turned around, came back, leaned over my desk and gave me two deep kisses in a row. Then with a big grin on his face he said: "I hope that's what you wanted." I told him I'd been waiting for that. I woke up incredibly happy and fulfilled. I have had multiple visits where I have asked for intimacy, and he delivered, and then verbally confirmed he was delivering what I asked. I get incredible comfort, confirmation, and fulfillment from these visits.

Threads

DREAM VISITS, IN WHATEVER FORM THEY TAKE, HAVE THREADS BACK to signs from your loved one. The signs are a pathway of comfort leading to a deeper meaning, a deeper connection that can come in the form of a visitation. It's like finding gifts along a trail that leads to the most beautiful place imaginable, where your loved one is waiting to deliver what your heart and soul needs.

I have found consistent elements that relate to conversations Roger and I had prior to his passing. We had in-depth conversations about how this was not the end, that this was only the start of our story, our journey. I find this in many elements of our dream visits. In most visitations, Roger is strong and getting stronger, physically healing or healed. There is always an acknowledgement of the heath issue, but it is in the past. We are moving on from it, everything is healing, we are on a path to recovery or fully recovered. There is an energy of wellness, and wholeness, and often a sense that I am protecting Roger while he completes his healing. There is a knowingness, often unspoken, that he is well. We get to do everything now, there is no holding back.

Invest in Your Relationship

WITHOUT CONSCIOUS THOUGHT, I IMMEDIATELY STARTED DOING the work, learning, and getting exposed to the tools and people who would help me connect. Some of tools and opportunities for learning that were put in my path really resonated with me because I was so lost. I am positive these tools were offered to help me navigate through for survival — to help me figure out what to do with the enormous weight I had on me. I felt so trapped and lost. I had never considered being without Roger. The fact that we did *everything* together made me feel even more confused.

What did I want to do? I had no idea. I didn't even know what I *could* do. I wasn't sure what I would or could do without him physically here. So much of what I enjoyed, I enjoyed because we did it together. I felt like I had to figure out who I was now. I certainly was not the person I used to be. What would be too painful to do now? What would I no longer want to do because I held it sacred for us, if it was only an *us* thing or place? There was so much to navigate. What would feel good? What would generate any semblance of joy?

Early on it felt like nothing would or could. Joy, when it did come, was random and oh so brief. Memories gave me the most comfort — our photos taking me visually back to our special places. This resonated with me and I am positive that it helped. I received nuggets and pulls from Roger and the universe right from the start.

Before Roger passed, I started to notice posts on the professional networking site LinkedIn from a spiritual coach who worked exclusively with women and focused on Akashic work. Akashic records are essentially the map of your soul throughout your lifetimes. I had no idea what that was, but her posts always spoke to me very deeply. I felt called to her. Soon after Roger passed, she posted images of the front of three tarot cards. Her post said to pick the image you felt called to you. I was immediately drawn to the card that ended up being titled The Goddess of Oneness. The next day, she posted the meanings, and the card I had chosen was so connected and true to what I was experiencing.

The Goddess of Oneness Oracle:

> *All in life is energetically (spiritually) interconnected but the strongest connection is between us and those we love and care for. You may be missing someone who is a long way away. Or alternately, you may be saddened by a loved one's passing. Through this card someone wants to make to make their presence felt. They want you to know that they have not left you and will never leave you, for you are forever connected by invisible threads of love. No amount of distance or time will ever change that which is united in love.*

> *Affirmations*

> *My love transcends all time and space.*

I am forever spiritually connected to those I love.

*Time and space does not exist within my soul."**

We are infinite beings who have chosen to experience a physical existence, and in doing so, we must experience the short sightedness and pain of not realizing we are surrounded by love. We believe we are alone; separate from others and the world; yet we are so much more connected than our limited senses perceive. Luckily, we are in a new millenia; one where we are able to photograph energy fields and expand our awareness of human consciousness. We are waking up to our power and just starting to comprehend our individual capabilities. Once we understand how powerful we are alone, we can band together to save the world.

Love is the key to all healing; it is also the key to opening our hearts to each other. When you experience fear, doubt, jealousy or suspicion, your heart chakra closes down and you can't properly send and receive love. When you trust, believe and have faith in yourself and others, your heart chakra opens up and you are capable of experiencing more love; which in turn raises your vibration. You can help those around you by setting the example of love, it's contagious!

This is a message from someone who loves you at a soul level.

(https://archangeloracle.com/2014/04/19/goddess-of-oneness/)

That was a tipping point; I scheduled a free virtual meet and greet. Her energy felt so healing and warm. It was exactly what I needed. I started working with her a month or so later. I'm not sure how other Akashi healers work, but for us, she took me into the Records with my guides. We did chakra healing work. She worked with her guide and mine to heal my current and past trauma. It was a very effective way to navigate my deep, deep grief.

We invest our time, energy, and healing into the relationships we have here in the physical realm. We need to make the same investments with our loved ones who have crossed. The phenomenal gifts, messages, and guidance they want to provide and bless us with are right there. We just need to clean the window so we can see them.

Regrets and second guessing are common during periods of grief. It could be a regret surrounding a loved one's passing. What if we had done this or that? What if he had driven this route that day? What if I hadn't asked him to pick up the dry cleaning? What if we had tried this treatment? Or gone outside of our country for experimental treatments? What if I had done this one thing differently to help with care? Would hospice have come later? Could we have bought more time? Could we have had one more birthday, one more Christmas, one more anniversary? Or you might replay arguments, quibbles, or other times you struggled in your relationship. This so hard because you so desperately want that time back — only 10 minutes would be the gift of all gifts.

Ultimately though, you will see — you will be shown — to release it. The timing was meant to be, as hard as that is for us to accept. This is especially true with the loss of someone young. There is a divine purpose, and divine timing is real. Once we trust, we get closer to the window and can see out, the "why" becomes clear. This is another reason to do the work. Investing in the spiritual work and connection brings you into communication with your loved ones and shows you the divine reason. It may be as simple as you would not have seen life the same way. You would not have seen the universe for all that it is, all that's possible. It is opening your mind and heart to the larger picture of all that is, all that connects to your soul and your true purpose on earth, in this body, in this lifetime.

Early on I made an important investment in learning. I listened to many audio materials that helped me connect to my inner strength. They may or may not have been spiritually themed, but they led me to that. They connected to me and to other teachings and there were many synchronicities. Many of these teachings were about being in your power no matter what. Building on and reinforcing inner strength, which I needed badly at that point. I was so torn up, so fragile that, depending on the minute, hour, or day, there were times when I didn't feel capable of moving forward.

Many of the books and podcasts I listened to had a central theme: live in the moment, live in the here and now. I did not take this to mean not connecting, and it did not take me away from visualizing and totally embracing our past. For me it meant don't worry about what next year looks like, or even next month or next week. I found quickly that nothing could tank me faster than thoughts of the future. Thinking about the future totally overwhelmed me. It made me want to give up. It brought thoughts of loneliness, confusion, lack of purpose, and not even knowing what I liked at the most basic level. It disempowered me, so I learned not to do it. There's a reason so many teachers, not even those related to grief, tell you to live in the present. The present is what matters, what's healthy.

I learned I could be present and carry my joy from the past with me. My joy, our joy could be in the present. I could tap into that favorite experience or place with Roger as a key part of being present. Meditation was and continues to be an excellent way to do this. Meditation made an enormous difference for me. I've discussed how meditation is a key part of my pre-bed routine. I also meditate in the morning, by I start my day with a walk, listening to 10-15 minutes of spiritually-based affirmations about connecting with source, being divinely guided in my best life. This helps ground me into what's important for the day. It also gives permission to my spirit to team up with my guides so they can help me as I move about my day.

If something happens during the day that is triggering or knocks me off center, I do a short breathing meditation focused on connecting with the source, God energy, and my spirit team. I start my deeper work at night. In addition to the pre-bed routine I've described, sometimes I listen to past Akashic recordings and prepare myself to have an awesome visit from my handsome hubby.

Songs

THE NIGHT BEFORE ROGER LEFT THE PHYSICAL WORLD, WE TALKED and kissed, and I played him a few songs. Sometimes I took off his CPAP mask, gave him a few kisses, then put it back on. Since we began dating, I always kissed him before bed: a kiss before bed, then he would say his prayers in his head. He told me he always prayed for me. One night we played the game: three kisses that resulted in a huge smile on his face. Then I sat next to him and played three songs, something I had not done while he was in hospice. Other nights we talked for hours about our adventures, our plans, our future, our love, our connection. But this night, the last thing I did was play three songs and my intuition called me, telling me to do the kissing game one more time. I feel that playing those songs for him that night was a rite of passage — a release for him to leave the physical. I think my soul knew. And I thank God I did. Those warm beautiful kisses will hold me through until we meet again in the non-physical realm.

The final song in my trio was one I had only listened to only once or twice before: "God Whispered Your Name" by Keith Urban. To the tune of this beautiful song, I offered my own prayer: *God whispered your name. I know you're being called. I know we made promises. I know we always keep our promises. Release your physical hurt and go to God. I know you are here no matter what. I know this is only the start. Three kisses. Then sleep.*

I was trying to get to Roger in time for the moment he passed from the physical world. I knew it was likely impossible. They say our last moments are the way our loved ones want them. Roger wanted three songs and three kisses to be our transition. As I scrambled to get in the car, to get there, my phone wouldn't connect to the car's Bluetooth. The car was silent — no phone, no music. In my panic, I was unaware of getting into the car or turning it on. About ten minutes later, out of the blue, my car started playing "God Whispered Your Name." I knew. I knew and this was my first sign. The first sign of many. I know that was Roger marking the time of his crossing and validating our final moments in the physical. He was letting me know it was okay and that this was the way it was meant to be. Three songs and three kisses.

Journals and Communication

DURING THE LAST FEW WEEKS ROGER WAS PHYSICALLY HERE, I started journaling everything. As soon as I walked out of the room for him to rest, I took notes. I often put notes in my phone. I had never been a journal person, but my soul knew this was the time to memorialize and hold close all the details. All the conversations, all the phone calls, all of the intentions, all of the love. I'm thankful for the knowing of this practice. I have every detail to come back to anytime I feel called. Anytime I doubt, anytime I am down or struggling, I can come back to those beautiful notes.

It also helped me set journaling as a practice. I started journaling all the signs, subtle and big, that I received. This was huge for multiple reasons.

If I had a day or hour or minutes when I was questioning or where I felt overwhelmed, where I let limiting thoughts of the future hold me back or distort my vision, I had those amazing signs to know and hold true. It also proved our promise. Roger always keeps his promises, so I could go back and see all he had been doing for me, all the validation of our continued relationship, partnership. This laid the foundation for what has become our amazing communication system.

Spiritual communication can start as a song, a bird, or a symbol. With recognition and trust it continues to build into this road map that allows you to continue to trust and grow a language.

Journaling also helps in moments of joy, light and strength. Journaling is there to come back to when you're in your deepest struggles, sadness, and depression. Journaling can help you reground, remind you, show you again what your soul knows. It's a wonderful way to shine a flashlight on the truth. By documenting critical elements of your story, even though you may just be wanting to or needing to focus on survival moment to moment, you are continuing to build your powerful story of love — the power of love to transcend all physical limitations, to help show you who you still are, to make good on the promise, to prove there is no death. There only is transformation.

Promises

DURING THOSE FINAL WEEKS, DAYS, AND MOMENTS IN THE PHYSICAL world, we repeatedly discussed and reaffirmed our intentions. It is our intent that we were — we are — forever. We discussed Roger finding me after he transitioned. I told him: "Find me after, promise you will find me." He always affirmed the promise, once with "damn right!" Roger is and was a man of his word. Reflecting back, the early messages and signs communicated that these were his affirmations that he was good, all was well, and that he was making damn sure I knew he would make good on our commitment.

Within weeks of his physical passing, I started receiving messages and visits. My first visitation dream came a few weeks after he passed. He was with me at our house, I was rubbing his shoulders and kissing him. I told him I loved him. There were other people around us, family, but I was the only one who saw him, the only one who knew he was there. I was just present with him. That was how we were in his final time here physically and how I was now. I had back-to-back visitations with him several nights that week in October. There were important messages in them, as well as connection. Sometimes I could audibly hear the messaging from him and sometimes I woke up in the middle of the night with important thoughts. The first visit I journaled was on October 27, 2020. The next night, we had another visit and I woke up in the middle of the night with the message "we are forever." The night after that he visited and I woke up to a phone text from Roger: "I love you, heart."

My phone was and is a tool Roger uses frequently to communicate with me. This was the first of many messages I would get from him via my phone.

I was just about to begin my work in the Akashic Records, and had multiple experiences between October 27-29. When I had my first session with my Akashic coach, she had never worked with anyone specifically looking for help to facilitate communication with someone on the other side. The work she did was to facilitate overall healing. I don't know if the Akashic work facilitated all my experiences, but Akashic work with the right healer is beautiful. I have a deep knowing Roger and I would have found pathways to build our language and communication system no matter what. I am forever thankful we set that intention.

Early in the morning of October 29, I had my first session with my coach who was based in the UK. Each session, she guided the experience, helping me work my way through my chakras at the start of each journey. Early on, my heart chakra was in much need of care and it was not unusual for me to cry at the start of a session. I was so raw at that point. When setting intention for the desired healing during the session, it can bring up a lot of emotion. It was very important for me to share the experiences I had been having on my own, especially since my coach would tap into my guides and angels to set the stage for my session. In each healing session, I dropped into a dreamlike meditative state, similar to a hypnotic state. I felt myself going through each guided experience, each healing detail that I was carried through by my guides. I frequently felt Roger in the sessions with me, as well, which made it even more beautiful and healing. Healing is a phenomenal gateway to opening yourself up to the other side. Deep pain that exists from your past can hold you back in ways you don't even realize. You can even hold grief as physical pain.

At the end of that first session, I felt like I was returning to the here and now, as if I had come back into my physical body. The session had ended and I was laying there still in a semi-meditative state. I looked over and could feel and see Roger right next to me, with his gorgeous blue eyes staring back at me, his head on the pillow next to mine. I reached over to push his hair back and we just looked at each other with complete love. It was so beautiful. I was so thankful for the gift of those brief moments.

The week of November 5 I had visits with Roger nearly every night. The message was always that he had come back to me. In one we were dancing, celebrating that he had come back. and we were both so joyful. In several visits over the following months, I was the only one who realized he was there. I was in the dream, and I knew we had this special bond, this magic, where he was present with me and it was just for us. That week, family started connecting with Roger's possessions, feeling closeness to him through his things. In these visits, I did not focus on the things. I was fully focused on Roger still being present. The signs continued to show up on my phone as well. The song "Soul," which I had never heard before, popped up on my phone. I felt it contained very specific messaging for me. The lyrics go "I like your soul baby, you've got that heart made of gold baby, I just want to be your baby." A few days later, my phone played the song "Cover Me Up," another song I had never heard before. It's a gorgeous country love song. A very soulful ballad, "so cover me up and know you're enough... 'cause somebody knew I was meant for you." Music was a big connection for us and the lyrics to both songs were relevant for us. When we first started dating, we frequently sat in his car for hours as he played music for me. We loved music, we shared music, we also often gave each other the gift of music in the form of concert tickets that sometimes included a weekend getaway to go to the show. Music was the link to his release, his transition, so it's fitting that he has these messages come to me in the form of song.

On November 10, I was particularly sad when getting ready for bed. Evenings often presented the biggest emotional struggle for me; I felt more alone in the quiet. This was often when I broke down and cried. As was my new habit, I meditated and looked at one of my favorite photos before going to bed. I had silenced my phone for the night and plugged it into the charger when I noticed the screen light up. An article popped up about the meaning of 11:11 and angel numbers, as well as the meaning of a Twin Flame, which was new to me. Twin flames are essentially one flame, one soul, split in two creating an extremely intense magnetic connection.

The following morning, unprompted by me, my Akashic coach told me that while consulting with the guides in preparation for my session, she was told Roger and I were twin souls (flames) or soulmates across many lifetimes. We have one soul split into two flames. which is part of why our bond was and is so tight. He had sent me the sign the night before and she was now confirming the date of November 11th — 11/11.

Guide

I HAD A SENSE THE SIGNS ROGER SENT WERE SPECIAL. IN THE physical world he looked out for me and showed me a rare love and compassion. He had a way of prioritizing my happiness. He constantly lifted me up. Here in the physical world, we always balanced each other. If one of us was down, the other would help lift them up. We played this role for each other naturally. We are both very positive people, looking for the benefit of every situation. From the other side, where it's pure love and light, Roger gives and shows love at a vibrational level.

My sense of this stronger ability for him to watch over me has been validated many times since his passing. My Akashic coach mentioned it first, telling me Roger acts as my high council. Your high council can be one or multiple guides on your spirit team that play the most elevated role in assisting you in this lifetime. They guide you for your soul's highest evolvement. I have since been told by several mediums that he leads my spirit team. Roger told me in sessions that part of the reason he gets to play this elevated role for me is because of our special relationship, our deep partnership of trust. I completely trust him and his guidance. During this early phase, I continued to receive messages on my phone, one of which stated that we are infinite souls in the human body. Other messages were centered around my growth and development, telling me I was in a critical phase of growth and to stay positive, to take it day by day. The simple act of focusing on the day by day creates positive change and improvement. The messages assured that things were developing for me even if they weren't visible to me yet. Looking back, the grief may have clouded some of my sight then, but I see now these changes were actually visible.

Throughout the November after Roger's physical passing, I had many dream visitations. Often his daughter Meghan was in the visit and many times there were core elements and messages that were consistent with other visits, such as our recurrent angel number (1111) and that he was healing or healed.

He also showed me elements only he and I knew, things we experienced together. He showed me what he was going through on the other side that was for he and I to know. Now I recognize these messages in his visitations. I'm sure they had to do with his review of his lifetime and the lessons he had as a result.

One afternoon in mid-November I was with our friend Maria, who had known Roger really well. She had cut our hair for years and had come to the house to do his hair when he was sick. Maintaining who he was, taking care of himself, was so important to Roger and her visits were meaningful. She is also very in tune with her intuitive powers. She and I were in deep conversation, talking about Roger, of signs, and she said she sensed him right behind me at that moment. Walking to my car, my phone popped up another song I had never heard titled "Wait for Me."

During late November I had beautiful visits with Roger, several of which allowed us intimate time. On one visit he walked in and put a beautiful heart-shaped card on the counter with a handwritten note and gift. The dream visits picked up communication from our day and were consistent with what was happening in the physical world. It was not uncommon to have more than one visit in a night. Sometimes when a visit was interrupted by me waking up, it picked up where we left off when I went back to sleep. On some dual visits, one allowed him to give me messages, love, and connection, and the other provided a visit or message for the kids.

Protection

In late November, as I referenced previously, several individuals tried to take advantage of our grief and take over the company Roger was so passionate about. We had lived and breathed the success and challenges of the business since it launched in 2008. It was our baby. I was even more passionate about the company after Roger's passing because of what it had meant to him. His kids and I fought hard for more than 90 days. During this tumultuous time there were many signs, messages, and visitations from Roger related to our efforts. I'm confident the ideas or knowing of things that showed me what to do or how to handle situations came from otherworldly sources.

I had several visitations with Roger where we were at work or a work event or conference. Mirroring our habits in the physical world, we enjoyed our alone time after being "on" for the event. We never strayed far from each other, loving to watch each other talk, network, and be on our game, in action with a room full of opportunities. When the vote for the company was getting close and I had been working to align resources on our behalf, I started seeing a new sign from Roger, messages of hawks in the sky, hawks following me or circling me on walks, hawks flying a foot or so over my shoulder. I began to see them all the time circling me on the trail I walked daily. They flew tree to tree alongside me. I knew right away this was Roger. He loved birds of prey: hawks, eagles, osprey. We had one at our last house that occasionally perched on our roof line, and he would go out to watch it and take photos. On our travels to Jackson Hole, he frequently talked about the beautiful osprey he saw while fly fishing. He loved seeing them hunt over the gorgeous barley fields. I knew that through these hawk signs he was telling me that he had me in this difficult time. He was giving me extra strength, empowerment, and protection, and telling me to continue to trust my instincts.

Hawks have been a constant sign for me from Roger ever since, a sign to trust. The hawk signs come consistently from Roger whenever a decision needs to be made or major events are occurring, as a way to confirm the road I'm traveling on. They are beautiful reflections and representations of how Roger is and always has been with me, giving me love, protection, and the freedom to fly.

Maddy

ROGER AND I HAD AN ADORABLE YORKIE GIRL I RESCUED WHILE WE were dating named Maddy. Maddy was every bit a terrier female. At whopping five pounds, she took crap from no one, and all of my boy dogs were terrified of her when she was on a tear. She was the sweetest little girl with us, and the boys adored her, but she always kept them guessing. She loved to cuddle up with Roger, sometimes giving me the side eye, like "he's mine." Many times, when he was sick and in hospice, Roger wished she was cuddling with him. We had lost her in January of 2017. For a puppy given very low odds of surviving when I rescued her at six months, the fact that she made it almost 14 mostly-healthy years was awesome. I was so happy and it felt so right when in mid-December of 2020 I had my first dream visit where Maddy was with Roger. He was healthy, she was healthy, and they were visiting me. He was talking to me about "his dog." He referred to Maddy and then Dallas, as "his dogs" when we were all here physically.

Throughout this week I had several visits with Roger where he let me know he was returning to me. There was communication and knowing that we would always be here for each other. He also started to show me concepts of bringing in other people to surround me and help me — people to help with the business. He showed a vision of me alone in a large circular room, then of him drawing others into the room. This was our circle of trust. I trust him implicitly, always have, always will.

Many of his visits over the coming weeks involved intimacy, showing each other love and care, spending time together, showing each other affection. Love, caresses, kisses, knowing we were intimate no matter what happens physically.

There is this connection at a cellular level in these other dimensions where you just feel, you know you had the experience. You may feel or just know what your body felt. You may feel or just know what was said. Like you are being rinsed from the inside with beautiful shining light of joy. That joy stays with you as you wake into the physical world.

Around this same time, I started receiving communications that Roger wanted me to share with his kids, and the first one was for Meghan. This particular night I had several dream visits with Roger. In them he was healthy again and we were at a work event together but carving out our own time. He told and showed me that we were alone in our bedroom on the bed talking and showing each other love when Meghan called. I could tell what was being said in the conversation from listening to him. She played a song for him. She was going to play more songs, but he stopped her and said: "It's okay to listen to the music I listened to, but I don't want you to listen to it so much that when you hear it you get sad." The next day, I talked with Meghan and at the end of the call I told her about the dream visit. I told her exactly what Roger said to her in the visit. She went totally silent and gently started crying. She told me that she listened to his music often before bed and the night before she had listened to song after song, sobbing and talking to her dad. It was so amazing; there was so much synergy and synchronicity.

Christmas

CHRISTMAS OF 2020 WAS SO SOON AFTER ROGER PASSED. I NEVER for a second thought he wouldn't be physically here for the holidays that year. In fact, I never thought he would not be here physically, even when he was sick and in hospice. Now, on some level, I think that was my soul's recognition of the forever of our presence together. It does not require physical union here in this realm.

The holidays hit while I still numb, still totally shell shocked. I was in total survival mode, only able to focus on keeping myself upright. But deep in the back of my mind I did have thoughts, probably subconscious, of what Christmas would look like without him. We went all out with our Christmas gifts for each other, doing something very meaningful, a gift or experience, that would really touch our partner — totally from the heart.

I loved thinking about the perfect gift for Roger. I loved his reaction of sheer happiness and joy. I knew him so deeply, and understood what the gifts meant and how they resonated. He was the same with me. His gifts had so much deep meaning. What would this year hold? He was my person; I always held what he gave me sacred. How would I get through this year without giving or receiving from the most important member of my soul family?

The Friday night before Christmas, Roger made sure that was not going to be a concern. I had a dream visit with him where our puppy Dallas was with us, and we were petting him. Then we were kissing and holding each other. We had a beautiful time together. The next morning my dad called said: "Your husband visited me last night and woke me up at 4:00 a.m." I frequently wake around 4:00 a.m. from a dream visit: specifically at 3:33 or 4:44. My dad told me Roger gave him a very special message, a present he wanted my dad to give me from him. Roger had showed him details of what the present should look like. My dad had told Roger that he would try, but we were down to the wire as this was the last shopping day before Christmas. Given the specifics of Roger's request, I think my dad was worried he would not be able to come through. When the spirit of our loved one on the other side sends a message they want acted on, they help with divine nuggets when we try. I told my dad that Roger had visited me that night as well. I now realize the irony that Dallas was in my visit with Roger since Dallas was a birthday gift from Roger.

My dad had less than two days to make Roger's present happen. Christmas Eve, I went to his house, and I opened what was clearly a jewelry box to find the most beautiful, sweet little silver angel pendant. This angel was so divinely feminine and absolutely represented what Roger thought of me and would have chosen for me. My dad said Roger showed him in his visit what the angel should look like. In the visit, when the jeweler took out two angels to show my dad, he immediately recognized the angel Roger had showed him. When my dad went to the jeweler to carry out Roger's wishes, they had zero angel pendants, but the owner thought he could get one or two later that same day. I've never heard of a jeweler getting an item for you on the same day, let alone right before Christmas. My dad referred to the jeweler by name: Tom as he told me the story of getting the necklace. I said "Tom L?" With a look of surprise, he said: "Yes, why?" When I told him that Tom was the one jeweler Roger used for my gifts, he was completely shocked. So many beautiful signs. That Christmas Day, my mom and I drove by the golf course Roger and I played all the time. As we approached the song "God Whispered Your Name" started playing. I thanked Roger for always making sure Christmas was extra special even from the other side.

Request

WE ALWAYS MADE THE HOLIDAY SEASON EXTRA SPECIAL. THAT YEAR, I continued to see angel numbers every day, and always his extra special one of 11:11. After six visits in eight nights, all meaningful, I was and remain filled with gratitude. I credit these visits with helping me survive. I started talking to Roger with specific intent before sleep each night, thanking him, telling him how incredibly grateful I was for his love, to the universe for facilitating and enabling our amazing partnership, and for opening myself up to receive him at night.

On the night of December 26, I did something for the first time, I told him I missed kissing him and asked for a kiss if he could visit me that night. I set the intention, but of course was not even sure we would have a visit. That night I did indeed have a visit. As I mentioned in previously, he did in fact kiss me. What I asked for actually happened *and* he called out that I requested it during the visit! This is one example of many, but it shows we can ask for specific things, signs, dream visits, we can make request and they are in fact heard by our loved ones.

This visit was transformational for me and my spiritual awakening. I knew the power of our words, our thoughts, and our intentions. This visit made me fully realize the power of intention. The power of us communicating what we need to our loved ones. The power of the possibilities of our communications and actions.

I speak to Roger all day, every day, mostly in my mind. At night, I talk out loud, sending my intention and attention. I focus my attention on gratitude and thankfulness for so many magical and amazing blessings. I focus my intention to clear my mind and open myself up to receive signs and messages from God/the source, my spirit team, and my phenomenal soulmate. Your words, thoughts and request matter. They are being heard and your loved ones want to help. As a gentle reminder, we have free well and your loved ones respect that so in order to get help, visits, or request we need to remember to invite them in. Ask for their help. Ask for their signs. Ask for their visits. Us setting the intention matters, we are opening the door for them to help us with what we need or desire.

New Year, New Sign

EVEN WHEN TRAVELING, I WAS ABLE TO CONNECT AND HAVE SEVERAL dream visits over the New Year's holiday. I got out of town intentionally to spend time with family, I guess as a sort of distraction. I had brief visitation connections with Roger on New Year's. This felt particularly amazing because it can be more challenging for me to make these connections when I'm out of my routine. I had not been sleeping well, either which made it more challenging. I need to enter into deep sleep for optimum conditions for visitations. Other than an occasional glass of wine or specialty beer every once in a while, I have never been a drinker. Alcohol tends to put a mask on sleep; it tricks the mind and creates a fake deep sleep.

On New Year's Eve, I had a short visitation and was lucky to have a full visit on the next several nights. Given the importance on New Year's to us, it was not surprising Roger picked this week to launch a new, amazing sign. New year, new sign. On January 3, 2021 my phone "randomly" told me I needed to call Roger. This sign popped up on my screen when my phone was shut off. I was not doing anything on the phone, I had not modified anything, I had not created anything new in my calendar, I never use reminders, and I had not added notes. Every day, at various times for more than a month, the sign came up on my phone, always with intention, always after some thought of mine about him or us, or when I had just been talking to him. One day in mid-February, it suddenly stopped. I got really upset and was crying, asking him if I was doing something wrong. I asked him if I had done something to screw up or if we just weren't doing that sign anymore? I asked that question as I was getting into my car. As I did, the reminder to call Roger popped up on my phone as a song of ours started playing.

And then the reminder ended. It ended and again this was pivotal to me. I learned through this sign, this experience, to trust more. Signs change, grow, develop, and pivot into new ones. This does not mean I did something wrong, that I didn't meditate, didn't get enough sleep, or that I said something wrong. This change and trust building was absolutely critical to my development, to growing our communication system. This experience also helped me let go of specific signs and the way they develop. I learned to trust in the knowing he is here always. No matter what the method, the beauty is that the magic exists, and it is and always will be with me.

Joy

IN EARLY-TO-MID JANUARY, I STARTED RECOGNIZING ROGER'S presence without specific messages or remembrance during the night. I often woke between 3:00 and 4:00 a.m. with a knowing of Roger's presence. These visits warmed up my day. I woke up smiling with a total sense of joy. I was still receiving the call reminders when I experienced my first presence visit. I even had a reminder to call Roger both in the early morning and late afternoon the following day when I journaled my first visit of this type.

I constantly had full dream visits, often with others we loved. Roger's daughter Meghan was regularly part of the visits. Maddy also found her way into many visits that month. And as we worked to save the company Roger had worked so hard to create, I had visits of us together at work having meetings, going to events, and traveling.

There has always been consistency to my visits with Roger, of him being present with me and pulling in elements from what is currently going on in my physical world. Details from the physical world, sometimes small or things you and I wouldn't focus on but resonated in the details as Roger's way of confirming he is always present with me. He listens to my thoughts and is aware of what's going on in my life. Many of these elements pull through in my visits with him. And sometimes, just as in the physical realm, the smallest thing creates the biggest joy. It can be the little things that resonate most with our soul.

For instance, I've woken from knowingness dream visits and smelled him so strongly — the specific aftershave balm he wore as a cologne that no one else wears. Smelling that is amazing, it gives me the biggest smile when my heart and soul already feel and know he was present with me. There is so much beauty and joy in waking to those moments. Those joyful feelings live deep within me, carrying me. He brings me so much — thankfulness, deep peace, and belonging at a soul level with him.

Stronger

MANY OF MY DREAM VISITS IN THE EARLY MONTHS HAD ELEMENTS that recurred. Many times, Roger was growing stronger, regaining his physical abilities. Many times, there was a sense of comeback or renewal, of his building his way back, a sense that he would come back to his full abilities or physical strength through a healing period. There was a strong element, often felt not spoken, of Roger transitioning into a new healthy version of himself, that he was going through rest and healing to be fully back. Often the kids and I were the only ones who knew he was back and healthy. In this deep reunion, there was always a sense of pure, amazing joy that he was able to come back to us, that the miracle and magic was true. There is a deep belief that he is always with us, one hundred percent present. The healing aspect resonated as him being early in his transition to the other side, and that he was healing from physical traumas so he could join us again as his full, beautiful, healed, higher self. There was recognition that we had been able to create and connect with the magic of our relationship after his transition, to experience our union fully. In some small but powerful way, I've been given the gift of bearing witness through his messages, our collective experiences, and our dream visits.

He is guiding me and bearing witness to my life, as well as showing me and telling me, directly, through signs, and through mediums, that he is aware of all facets of my life. He is especially aware of my thoughts, which are often in direct conversation with him. This is not just a one-way street. I also can see, feel and be part of what changes, experiences, thoughts, and consciousness are part of his journey on the other side. In this way he gained strength, I gained strength and, most importantly, we grew stronger in our union. We elevated our bond and our partnership past the simple three-dimensional physical world to include the dimensions of time and space.

We get to experience together what many experts speak of as a rise in consciousness. Even for just a few hours here and there, it is an amazing gift. I can't fully express how visceral my happiness is when I see and more importantly know his strength and love for all of us, to know that he is back, and he is here. Each time I have one of these dreams I feel with every cell of my being an unbelievable elation at being reunited. In our waking hours, we all sometimes wonder what it would be like if a loved one who has passed suddenly walked through the door, pulled in the driveway, or just showed up where we are. These are insanely powerful emotions, the happiest bliss one could ever know. That deep, real bliss lives in our meeting places. It is real, always linked to my waking life, and the most important true experience for us.

Signs in Twos

As I went back through my journals to write our story, I noticed the synchronicities of signs and the times when signs bled into one another. For example, I found a printout of a gift I had given Roger, a trip to Green Lake. This is one of the places I take myself to be with him when I do meditation visualizations. One day in early February 2021, before I even started that practice, I was cleaning my desk and found the printout I had given him for the gift, with gorgeous color photos of the golf course, detailed information on the resort, the restaurants I booked, and the dates. I was excited to find it and I knew he had guided me to it that day to give me joy. I keep that printout in a special place on my desk to bring me joy each day.

As I placed it on my desk, I was instantly taken back to our experiences at Green Lake. A few hours later, out of the blue, a full montage of the Green Lake trip popped up on my phone. A few days later, a reminder to call Roger popped up on my phone just seconds after seeing a car just like the one he drove, which was not a common car.

Another time, as I was driving past our favorite golf course, a favorite song of ours played for me at the same time that an article about twin flames popped up on my phone and the clock turned 11:11.

Intentional Expansion

IN MANY WAYS, BOTH THROUGH MEDIUMS AS WELL AS IN DREAM visits, I've been told that Roger's passing had to happen, that the timing and the way it happened needed to be exactly as it was for our souls' growth, for my purpose, and many other reasons. Roger touched everything in my life, and there has been a spider web effect in everything I've been pulled to since he transitioned. On one visit in particular he communicated with me that the timing and reason for his passing was also related to my relationship with his two kids. The three of us have been through so much together and we are incredibly close. Roger communicated with me that all of these hard things, events, and experience, were, in part, to give us the path towards that deep bond.

Roger often told or showed me the important elements of relationships. This was especially true at the beginning, when there were huge struggles with the business and the stresses of such deep grief. He previewed experiences and conversations with individuals who might challenge us. Some were friends I had not talked to in years, but they came and said something I needed to see, understand, or know to heal, forgive, or build deeper bonds.

In the first segment of one two-part visit, Roger was healed. We kissed and talked about getting a new house. There was a peaceful renewal about the visit. We enjoyed our time together, laughing, telling jokes, sharing important conversations, and bonds. In the second part, I received a message that I did not know at the time was for Meghan. Roger's mom is also on the other side with his father. This was the first time his mom had been in a visit, and she has only been in a few since. Roger's dad was pushing her in a wheelchair. The four of us were talking and his mother, Marilyn, got upset about something. Roger asked me what upset her. It turned out she was panicked because she lost something. I couldn't understand what she had lost, but it was something very meaningful to her. We were trying to settle her down and to help her locate the item when I woke up.

These two visits were like multiple layers of experience, carrying into my waking day and the next evening. I called Meghan the next day, and we were all over the board in our conversation, per usual, something Roger used to tease us about. At what I thought was the end of the call, I mentioned the previous night's dream visits. I told her that her grandmother and grandfather were there and how her grandmother had lost something and was really upset about it. I told Meghan I was trying to figure out what it meant and she instantly started crying. She had lost her grandmother's engagement ring the night before, the same night I had the dream, and had just found it before our call.

Two-fer

ONE NIGHT I HAD A DREAM VISIT WITH ROGER WHERE HE WAS helping me right the wrong with the main individual who had tried to harm and take over the business. Roger and I were at the office and this person tried to go into one of the open offices. Roger had a "come to Jesus" moment with him behind closed doors. Meghan and I watched through the glass, very much wanting to back Roger up. I finally stepped in and the three of us escorted this individual out. We had been celebrating Roger's return before the drama started. Our celebration was so real. He was back in time for his upcoming birthday. We talked about how we needed to update the company website and social media, removing the memorial on our website since Roger was back. The dream visit was powerful and packed with many meaningful elements. The next day I had a session with my spiritual coach and told her about the dream visit. She likened the competition to a karmic reckoning, with Roger setting this person straight and releasing him from our future so we wouldn't have to encounter him again.

That same night, I had a second even more powerful visit with Roger. I was in my bathroom getting ready. The dogs were downstairs. I had just showered and put on makeup when he appeared and surprised me. I felt and knew every physical sensation from that romantic visit, it was beyond real. I woke up absolutely knowing we had been together. I had been upset the evening before, crying and grieving our physical connection. He showed up and gave it to me. I can pull from that visit just as well as I can from any memory that happened here in the physical world. It was a game changer for me — another layer of recognition of the miracles and magic that are possible.

Dream Inside a Dream

WHEN I AM ABLE TO CONNECT WITH ROGER IN A DREAM VISIT, WHAT we do in the dream and the messaging I receive is relevant to the physical world, but there is another interesting aspect as well. It is hard to describe, and I feel limited by language to communicate the experience, but essentially it feels like I'm having a dream within a dream. My conscious mind is fully aware of the connection both inside and outside of the dream. I feel it represents the true merging of worlds. We pull my knowingness and experiences from the physical world. Roger has proven that he is aware of each day and has the ability to adjust, create calm and confidence in me, or sometimes just clarity or beauty. Beauty in and of itself is essential and helps me in all ways on all levels. There is a gorgeous push/pull relationship between time and space. There is an influence and comfort, a limitlessness to what we experience, and a fluidity to our interactions. This carries seamlessly from waking to dreaming and vice versa. There is this awareness that the dream and my waking are of equal importance. More importantly, the dream influences waking life, not just in thought and confidence, but also in energy. The positive healing energy of being together in the dream state is just as strong and palpable in my waking state following the visitation.

I get to experience time and togetherness with Roger, and we are able to have conversations resolving the challenges I'm facing. He's able to give guidance that often comes in the form of healing. For example, he lets me know the information I need to release something that is stressing me out. Sometimes, when I have been fixated on something, or experiencing sadness or rejection, I can literally feel it release inside the dream visit and then outside it in the physical world. This feeling of vibration and energy has allowed me to move past issues and challenges with much more ease and grace than I ever have. It has accelerated my ability to get to a healthy, high vibe sense of release and flow. Once I feel it, feel what it's like within the 5D, I can release it with ease in the physical realm.

Sometimes I wake from a dream visit still in a somewhat altered state, similar to hypnosis or meditation, to an important message. I had such an experience the night of our wedding anniversary, when I woke to my Apple Watch and phone buzzing with a text from Roger: "I love you!" with the <3 symbol.

Interludes

Yoga

As runners and hikers, yoga and stretching were not our strengths. Roger was better at stretching post workout than I ever was, but he was notorious for not even making it through part of a movie without getting up and doing something or cleaning something. We decided yoga would be a great way to balance out our go go go workouts and lifestyle. It was way to relax more, something neither of us did very well. I started first, then convinced Roger, which consisted partly of telling him there were other guys there. I'm not flexible — I can get by in yoga, but that's it. Roger was even less flexible. He was starting to build a little base and able to modify moves since he had a hip replacement. After a few months of classes, the instructor knew us well, including the depth of seriousness we both brought to class, which is to say we swam at the shallow end of the yoga pool.

We were always matted next to each other, occasionally whispering together while trying to avoid dirty looks from classmates. Luckily the environment was much less intense than some studios or we would have been booted out after the first class. During one class, we were doing balance moves like tree pose, dancer pose, and warrior three. While working on pigeon pose, standing with one leg up and extended, we happened to be facing each other. Roger settled into the pose for a second then got wobbly, settled in, got wobbly, repeat. Finally, he held it for a few seconds and looked at me. He was thrilled to hold the position. I looked at him with a completely serious face and blew into the air... puff... little breeze headed his way to knock him over. He started laughing so hard, and that's how we did yoga.

Almost Free

Roger and I always had running jokes about the deliveries at our house. Whether it was Amazon or countless other online retailers I am not going to lie there were not a lot of days were they was not something delivered. Online has been my go-to for years, before Amazon prime became a huge thing. Part of the reason for me has always been priorities. I would rather spend my time being productive, be it work, working out, spending time with Roger, and or hanging with our pups. Shifting through items and potential finds at a brick-and-mortar store has never really been my jam. Given the number of items delivered and my propensity over the years to pull the trigger on things, not huge purchases but a good amount of items throughout the year, Roger loved to tease me. He would make comments like "every day is Christmas at our house." Or one year we were visiting my mom in Colorado for a long weekend, we were in the mountains, not a rural area but certainly not a dense population or a lot of stores, Roger and I were on a walk in her neighborhood. The houses were very spread apart with big, wooded lots, windy roads, and a mountainous back drop, as we walked up the hill to her house a UPS truck slowly drove by. Roger exclaimed, "Lindsay.. Lindsay... they found you! Don't worry baby they found you." The truth was he had so much fun with it and he loved when I bought new clothes in particular, he loved me showing them to him, he loved watching me try them on and put together a new outfit. So, he was admittedly an enabler. But that didn't prevent him from having fun with me about it. I used to always tell him what ever deal or sale I got when I would show him the new items. So, he started saying to me, literally laughing as he said it, "so it was almost free, I mean you had to, how could you NOT buy it." It became very much a running joke with us. Meghan would frequently be part of the joke or comments as well since she was very much the same in the online ordering department. Roger looped my friend Mary into it as well since she is not shy to buy either haha. So, when gifts have arrived since Roger's transition, like the items the second Christmas or just even smaller items I was thinking in my head, babe it wasn't almost free it WAS free and laugh. And when I know he would want me to pull the trigger and buy the thing I am desiring I think about him laugh and saying that expression to me, I visualize, feeling his presence in the moment, his validation to just do what would make me happy. Now days it tends to be more about investing in programs, sessions, teachings, and healings than "stuff". But sometimes, even though I know the "stuff" doesn't matter I just do the thing, buy the thing, because why not. Roger lived by the fact that tomorrow isn't promised, so don't save the thing, wait to do the thing, or most importantly show the act of love or kindness. Because that, well that is free, and it matters so, so much.

Gatsby

The Great Gatsby, circa 2013 starring Leo DiCaprio, was one of our favorite movies. Getting Roger to sit through an entire movie was rare; getting him to watch a movie more than once was a statistical outlier. *Gatsby* was an outlier. Roger was/is a true romantic at heart. The movie's costumes, the classic taste and beauty, the cars and fun music, made it a total win. The story of Jay's undying love for Daisy resonated deeply with us. We owned the movie and the soundtrack; we could recite lines from it. One late fall evening we were out for a walk as the sun was setting on the western trail. The trees were turning, the sky was blazing with a with the brilliant colors of sunset pinks, blues, and purples. We were taking in the clean, crisp fall air, joking, laughing, and feeling gratitude. Suddenly, I grabbed my phone and started doing the running man while walking to "$100 Bill" by Jay-Z from *Gatsby*. I was laughing at myself and Roger loved every minute of it. These types of random quirky acts were his favorite. His face and his body reflected total joy in that moment.

Some of the simplest moments of our time here on earth are the best. These simple memories can help you visualize deeply, to the point where you are back in that moment. The words pure joy are purposeful. Pure joy comes from the simple, the unforced, the uncomplicated.

The Future

I always open the door to Roger's guidance, giving permission and happily inviting him to assist or show me elements that he feels I need to see or feel. We also talk of the future, planning it and laying out aspects of our lives, just as we would if he was here in the physical world. We have discussed in detail new houses, the company, the kids, our dogs, and golf.

We frequently share the secret that we are the only ones in the know that he is back. If someone from the physical gets added to a dream visit and they have not been there before, there is often a message for me about that interaction. Roger and I have this knowingness, a communication, that the person is unaware Roger is here, and we know how that plays into our future. If someone had been at his celebration of life or read a memorial about him, it's like this code between us that they don't know that Roger is back. Some of the communication, a goodly amount, is telepathic. We may be expressing love, support, and comfort for each other in this way. We physically interact, but in addition to the physical, there is this telepathic knowing that I am always with and here for him and he is always with and here for me.

The visits and the signs layer into each other, further supporting this, showing how to communicate in any form. In many ways, the ability to connect and express are well past our limited ways of expression here in the physical world. Anything and everything is an opportunity for expression, connection, and communication with the other side.

I also see angel numbers dream visits and they can correlate with numbers sent to me that day or the next day in the physical realm. They may also correlate with numbers shown when I wake up and record a visit in my journal.

Validation for Them

AS I GO BACK THROUGH MY JOURNALS I SEE THAT THE VALIDATIONS are not just for me. They don't just validate for us in the physical world, we validate our loved ones on the other side. Our thoughts, requests, and actions even in a dream state can act as validation for them. In many visits I have validated for Roger that he looks strong, handsome, able, and healthy. I felt myself supporting his recovery. I validated his comeback, that his ability to be here while on the other side was deeply desired and that he was successful. I was receiving his healing energy, his strong and getting-stronger presence. In many visits I expressed to him how great he is doing, how amazing what he has managed to do is. I could see and feel his reaction, and the importance of my assurance of his success. I validated for him how magical it is and the enormous joy it has brought to me and the kids.

I have had several visits where I kissed him or hugged him or initiated intimacy, and I told him that I'd been dreaming of doing this for so long. I could see and feel his joy when I expressed that to him, which is also consistent with my desires and longing in the physical world.

Messenger

SEVEN MONTHS TO THE DATE AFTER ROGER PASSED, DIANA — MY closest female friend and second mother — passed suddenly and totally unexpectedly. After 16 years in the Jackson Hole area, she had just moved back home to Chicago in December; she passed in May. Many things had pulled her back to Chicago, but I know the move was largely influenced by Roger. While Roger was in hospice, Diana called to tell me she was considering moving back to Chicago, but wanted my opinion. I told her immediately I thought it was a great idea. Roger was resting during the call, but when he woke up he agreed it was a "splendid idea." Within days, she started making plans — talking to a realtor, looking at housing options, and having conversations around logistics. She wanted to be here for the holidays. Her kids, by birth, were in Chicago and another significant factor for her move was that her daughter had lost her spouse suddenly about six months before Roger passed.

Having Diana home felt right. She knew me so deeply. She was also very close with Roger, so it was an ideal time for her to come home. Her house sold extremely quickly, over a weekend, and the buyer preferred a quick closing. Diana wanted a quick close as well so she could start making the journey from Idaho to Chicago, a very long trip with two dogs as well. Luckily, she sold most of her furniture so that was one less thing to worry about moving. I had found a short list of places to look at for her to potentially buy. She found a great local realtor. There was one house in particular that seemed perfect, brand new and in a great over 55 neighborhood. She was excited about the idea of the community center and events they offered, especially coming from being in such a relatively isolated spot so far out in Idaho. Once she was here, we started talking about what we would do now that we were in the same state again! It had been so long. We made plans to go on a few little weekends trips the following year, all dog related. We had never been able to experience some of the historical dog shows with her because they were on the East Coast and she was too far away in Idaho/ Wyoming. When she settled into a wonderful new home in the Chicago burbs, she and I worked closely decorating the new place with the modern furniture she had always wanted. This was another benefit of not moving her furniture, she got to start fresh. I helped her find the car of her dreams. She was set up in a beautiful newly-remodeled home with plenty of new people to meet and things to do. She made it in time for Christmas, but she hadn't been feeling well. On Christmas Day, my mom was in town and the two of us drove Christmas dinner to Diana, visiting with her for the evening. I was so happy she finally had everything she needed and wanted. She had had health challenges over the years, but she was a total powerhouse who always bounced back. She had faced so much adversity in life, but always plowed through. Her strength and conviction were second to none. She was tough, beautifully strong and independent, and yet extremely loving and caring. She loved me like a daughter.

I was able to visit her several times in the months after she moved back and I talked to her most days, if not by phone at least by text. She had several hospital visits off and on over the months due to an infection in a joint replacement she had had back in Idaho. They had a hard time identifying and treating the issue, she would be in the hospital for a few weeks, get released and do home rehab and then start the cycle again. This happened several times before they finally gave her a strong enough or correct IV antibiotic to treat the infection fully in early spring. They also did a mini surgery as part of the treatment to open and clean everything out. She needed physical therapy to get her mobility back since they had opened her leg up the final time. She had the house set up well to accommodate her needs. And her daughter was taking care of the dogs during her recovery. After a few weeks the dogs were able to come home and settle in with their mom. And the house had been set up at that point for easy let out with a little fence area for them off the back patio. In order to help and make sure she had everything she needed a care giver Roger and I had worked with agreed to assist. He was actually able to stay with her for as many weeks as she needed while she recovered. I would talk with him, and he would always tell me what she needed and generally give me a very positive report consistent with hers on how great she was recovering. Her PT was going really well, and she was getting much stronger. We had the conversation about her actually winding down the need for her care giver. On May 1st, a Saturday, in the evening she and I talked for a long time. I offered to come over the next day but also told her if she wanted to rest, we could wait and I would come to celebrate Mother's Day the next weekend. She thought that was best, we said I love you like we always did at the end of our call. She pretty much always referred to me as kiddo at the end of our calls. I loved talking to her about all the important details of my life. She always remembered every important detail. If we had a work trip coming up, she would remember the exact dates and where I was going. If Roger and I had something fun planned she would bring it up ahead recalling exactly when it was. Even the little things most would not think important to pay attention to or remember, she paid attention to them, she remembered them. She loved talking to me about Roger and we loved talking about the amazing signs and communication he provided me after he transitioned. I honestly, reflecting back, think she expected it. She knew our bond and connection better than most.

The morning of May 2nd her care giver called me and said she wasn't feeling well, and she seemed really off. He told me he thought he should take her to the hospital and asked if that was ok. I told him absolutely and to keep me posted. That call was mid am. I texted and called a few tines for an update but wasn't surprised I hadn't heard yet as I assumed she may get admitted, also with covid protocols at that time it was a slower process to check in. At little afternoon, I had just returned from a walk and was in my kitchen about to prep lunch, when I got a call from her daughter. I will never forget the details of that conversation. She started by saying "have you heard." I said no, was she admitted? She then told me she passed. I literally dropped to the floor in my kitchen. 7 months to the day after Roger passing Diana passed. I was in total disbelief. I still am actually. Having been hit both enormous, traumatic losses, transitions, in such an incredibly short time frame in many ways I don't think allowed me to go through the grieving process properly with Diana. I know I still have work to do on her transition. I am thankful she was home, I am thankful we made fun plans for the future, I am thankful we spoke the night before, and I am thankful she knew I was open and ready to receive signs.

Right after she passed, she came to me in a brief but powerful visitation. She was validating to me that she was doing great and all was well. She walked up to me and handed me a box. As I was opening it, I looked up to see her, but she was already gone. The box held a gorgeous colored glass rose. Roses were her deal. She always grew gorgeous roses even in less-than-ideal climates and soil. Even when it was hard for her physically care for them, she prided herself on her beautiful roses. She loved all flowers and had enjoyed going to the big flower and garden show at McCormick Place in Chicago each year before she moved to out west. For her memorial, we got a breathtaking urn with embedded flowers and roses. We had a rose cake for her celebration. The rose she gave me was an important symbol, validating for me that she was well.

The second visit from Diana was very cool, tying together messages and signs from Roger. They were close friends here in the physical world — my joint cheerleaders. She was the one I talked to all the time about the daily signs, gifts, and visitations from Roger once he was on the other side. When she visited me, it tied that all together. In the second visit, she walked up to me, opened my hand, put something in it, and walked away. I opened my hand as I watched her leave; she had placed a beautiful frog figurine in my hand. Frogs were one of Roger's signs. She loved when he somehow delivered — manifested — a concrete frog to me soon after his passing. She thought that was so cool, so Roger, so the way he showed his love for me. She and I would talk about how in my deep grief, at one of my lowest points this precious cement frog showed up in my yard. She was in awe of what Roger was able to do to give me comfort and love from the other side. How he could use signs like the frog to communicate with me and let me know he was watching over me, hearing me, and loving me from the other side. Now, she pulled it all together in a beautiful package with a bow on top and a frog inside.

Work Nuggets

IN LATE MAY, RIGHT BEFORE ROGER'S BIRTHDAY, I HAD BEEN working on a contract with a large prospect for the company. We had tried to sign them as a client before, and Roger had been part of those meetings. I was excited about this deal as it represented significant revenue for the business, which was particularly important as we tried to recover from the damage done following Roger's passing.

There were signs and synchronicities along the way with this prospect; meetings verified at angel number times, for example. One of the meetings with key executives was booked at 11:11 for example. Another example was on his birthday receiving a very important email from the prospect with major indicators they would buy. Many elements of the prospect relationship felt particularly nudged. I had a dream visitation with Roger where he told me if I signed this prospect, he was going to give me a certain gift, a financial incentive. He talked with me in detail about the prospect and how to close the deal. He used to do that sometimes in the physical world, create little contests or incentives. The day after the dream visit, I was scheduled to get my first COVID shot. I have had anaphylaxis from vaccinations in the past, so my friend drove me to the appointment. At the time, the vaccines had only been available for a month or so, which made getting an appointment a challenge, so my appointment was about 40 minutes from my house in an area I do not normally visit. I remember my friend's GPS taking us this weird way and we commented on it, wondering why we on were these windy backroads rather than the highway. Signs were on the way. I told her about the previous night's visitation and suddenly there was a huge building with a sign for the prospect that I was trying to bring on board. I didn't even know they had offices in the area. We both got a huge smile and within the next few days, I closed the account. And a totally unexpected check came in the mail following the account becoming a customer.

Back to the Future

SOME SIGNS ARE SO BIG THERE IS NO WAY TO MISS THEM. WHEN they come, I picture my loved ones on the other side laughing like "she has to get this one!" Sometimes when I am doing a mundane task, the sublime occurs and offers a huge light of beauty from the other side.

For two nights leading into Roger's birthday, we had wonderful visits and I was lucky enough to have a wonderful dream visitation with Roger on the night of his birthday. This visit had many little Easter eggs tucked into it, carefully placed messages about conversations we'd had before he passed, information around our connection, and conversations I had recently had with my spiritual coach. We had just had this time together, this ability to connect in another dimension.

The day after his birthday, I was on my way to the car dealer for some maintenance work, on a route I drive frequently. I stopped at a light and looked at the car immediately in front of me. It was a *DeLorean* — a *Back to the Future*, batwing-style-doors DeLorean. The license plate read "Time Lord," which I Googled. A Time Lord is a character capable of manipulating and traveling between time, of course. I had a huge smile with total knowing that this was a sign Roger sent for me — a powerful sign in and of itself, as well as a validation of the many visits I had experienced in the days leading up to that.

Playlist

THROUGHOUT LATE SPRING I HAD REGULAR DREAM VISITS, MOST weeks experiencing at least one. They continued to help me so much. I had developed my pre-bedtime routine to help release the clutter and stressors of my day from my mind, to help clear the path. I experienced daily signs as well. Like a lot of the messaging, they were establishing patterns or paths to get me to recognize and trust.

Butterflies have been a very consistent sign for us, and I was seeing and experiencing them almost daily when no one else that lives by me was seeing them at all. One of my friends who lives about half a mile from me had planted specific flowers to try and attract them to her house and she wasn't seeing any at all. I, on the other hand, saw them daily on my morning walks, in the evening when I was walking the dogs, in the yard, and even when in my car running errands. I had them land on my hand. I saw them in little clusters, even monarchs. Sometimes I saw a shadow of one and then another would fly around me. These signs were always validating, always there, in combination with all the other amazing signs and visits They helped me keep putting one foot in front of the other.

Anytime I got too low in my grief, I tried to pull myself up with a reminder of all the nuggets I was receiving. These amazing blessings that were floating in each day and each night. I looked forward to each night and the potential of seeing Roger. I am forever thankful for all these gifts.

I have heard mediums and spiritual healers say how much those on the other side will leverage other people, pets, events, and places to get messages through. I have experienced that our loved ones' love is stronger when we share their stories and the signs they send with others. They seem to get motivated and send even more. It's like a recognition and sign of gratitude that we are excited to share the experiences with others.

One evening I was in my yard with the boys — my dogs — and my neighbor invited me to hang out on her patio. She and I have had awesome conversations around past lives, communication, and signs from the other side. That night I went over and we talked and shared spiritual stories for hours. She had music playing in the background, a playlist of "random songs" from Pandora. At a certain point I had to stop and say something. When we were dating, Roger and I often went for a run in the evenings and then jumped in his car and talked for hours while he played his favorite songs for me. Every one of the songs on this "random" Pandora playlist was a song he played for me. Every single song.

Always Present

IN MULTIPLE DREAM VISITS, ROGER'S MESSAGE IS THAT HE IS ALWAYS with me, always protecting me, always going to be here for me, and always loving me. I've had others come up to me in dreams and share the same message, that I should not worry, that Roger is here and will always be here for me. Sometimes that is the entire intent of a visit.

Daytime Visitation

BY LATE SUMMER, I HAD BEEN VERY MUCH COMMITTED DAILY TO MY spiritual practice, investing time in our relationship and loving the communication systems we had started to build. I had begun following a podcast by a spiritual teacher. At the end of each episode, she walked through a light visualization, a oneness meditation. It was something I could do while walking or doing some small task. The purpose of the mediation was to connect and feel the connections of our energy with all other beings, plants, animals, and loved ones, here and on the other side, as well as with our angels and the source/God. I found this mediation beautiful; I loved the open and grounded state it put me in. I experienced short visualizations with Roger right after doing this meditation.

I have a deep knowing that what I have heard other spiritual teachers say is true: if we see an image of our loved one or a memory flashes through the screen of our mind, that is our loved one visiting us. I also firmly believe when we set our intention on thinking about and seeing our loved one, we are calling them to visit us.

This was just before my stepdaughter's wedding. When finished the oneness meditation, my phone suddenly started playing an Elton John song I had never heard before. It was a current remix of one of his original songs. Roger and I loved Elton John. One of the last concerts we went to before Roger passed was Elton John and it was epic. We had been to many concerts over the years, but we agreed this was tops. This remix was super catchy, with a faster tempo than most of his songs. With the song came an amazing visualization. I could see from the first touch of our fingers to the final series and kiss a fully choreographed and amazingly cool dance between Roger and I. I had a total knowing we were at Meghan's wedding, and we had just surprised everyone with this dance. There was a sense of everyone \watching the love pour out of us as we danced. The choreography was so cool. As the song ended, we completed the dance and the visualization ended. It was amazing; I felt we had performed this flawless dance. it was such a wonderful experience, and I was awake during every moment. As the experience ended, a very large Monarch butterfly circled me and disappeared. I felt that was validation that this gorgeous dance just happened.

Ask and You Shall Receive

Only a few months after Roger passed, Netflix released a new series titled "Surviving Death." I felt a calling and received the signs to watch it. The series itself was very helpful. When I was in grade school and high school, I was extremely interested in near-death experiences, or NDEs. I read all of Doctor Raymond Moody's studies of NDEs. The Netflix series started about NDEs and progressed from there. The timing and information in the series was very helpful and it drew me to an excellent resource that ended up being a phenomenal tool in my toolbox — the Forever Family Foundation (FFF). The series featured FFF on the third and fourth episodes. They showcased several of the mediums who had been through an extremely robust vetting process for certification from FFF. The series featured the first medium FFF certified, Laura Lynn Jackson. Jackson's book *Signs* is an extremely powerful resource for anyone on their journey to connection.

The series also featured segments of the certification process for the mediums. FFF is a nonprofit and the founders built it with the sole purpose of helping people through traumatic grief. The husband-and-wife founders, The Ginsburg's, had experienced the sudden passing of their daughter when she was a child. They saw the huge gap in resources to help people navigate through such traumatic pain and that was the impetus for the creation of FFF. I was intrigued by the mediums and the opportunity to secure a reading from someone who was vetted and trusted, and learned about the special grief retreat FFF hosted once a year. The retreat hosted a limited and intimate group, always in the same remote location. The series gave a sneak peek into the experience s and interviewed several attendees. I was very drawn and knew I had to become a member of the foundation and try to attend this grief retreat.

The series was a top ten hit across Netflix for months, and with a mere 50 spots open for the retreat, I knew it would fill up as soon as the registration went live. I have no shame in admitting I stalked my email and the site for the announcement. I registered minutes after it opened and got in. FFF ended up adding two more events later that year in new locations because of the large following from the series. Attending that event was hugely important for me. It helped me connect back to myself, and I even experienced the first snippets of joy and life I had felt in a long time. The sessions were all performed by talented leaders in their field, all volunteers who just wanted to help those suffering and in deep pain. The lessons and content were wonderful and cathartic, but the people I met and the friendships I made were priceless. These were individuals who all got it; no explanations needed, only total love, support, and community with each other.

I also got to meet a medium certified by FFF, Joe Peretta. The reading with Joe was the first I had following Roger's passing. I am a firm believer, that part of getting a powerful reading is about having an energetic match with the medium. The medium should match the personality and energy of your loved one on the other side if possible. My reading with Joe was virtual and as soon as he logged on and started making small talk, I knew Roger would love his energy and vibe. I was able to talk with Roger through Joe for more than 40 minutes. (Roger did allow a few others close to me to come through.) I had spoken to Roger daily since he passed and had already experienced so many validations of signs, messages, and conversations from him. The reading gave me so much confidence and confirmation of what already I recognized that I was in fact receiving all of these messages from Roger. Roger was super proud of himself for some of the really big signs he was able to send to me, particularly amazing ones including the DeLorean he validated through Joe. The reading was awesome and magical.

At the grief retreat several months later, I met Joe and the rest of the spectacular FFF crew for a life altering experience. Though it seems weird to say, I felt lighter after attending the grief retreat, being there with so many— mediums. A select few attendees got impromptu readings. The "Happy Medium," Kim Russo, a famous and completely beautiful soul, was one of the educators that weekend. Kim is amazing. She taught a session energy and intuitiveness, teaching us to use vibrations and connecting energy to tap into our intuition and knowing. The session started was in a big open room with chairs set up in a circle. Kim's chair, at least what I predicted would be Kim's chair, was at the top of the circle. I was the second person to arrive of what ended up being about 20 people. I first sat next to the chair I thought Kim would be in, but the only person in the room before me was an older woman I had become friendly with; she and her daughter were at the retreat together and she asked if I would mind giving the spot to her daughter. I happily moved to the bottom of the circle.

Most of the chairs were conference type chairs except at the bottom of the circle there was a small loveseat and next to it a high-backed, overstuffed armchair. I went straight to the chair. What I did not realize, but am totally confident Roger did, was that it was directly under a skylight. It was a bright sunny July day and the sun was shining right on me,

essentially lighting me up. Additionally, I was now directly in
Kim's line of vision. No matter what, she would be looking
at me. Soon she came in and introduced herself, and told
us what she was going to teach. She stopped before she
going further, stared at me and said from across the room:
"You seem so familiar." She said she felt as if she knew me.
She made that comment a second time during the teaching
session. Most mediums, at least in my experience, will
preface a reading, particularly an impromptu one and they
say something to the effect of you have a sister on the other
side or a grandmother, etc., As soon as the lesson was over,
Kim looked at me, into my soul and said: "I see your heart
split in half. I see your soul split in half. The other half of
your heart and soul is on the other side; you're split in two."
The intensity and raw power of the reading continued. She
knew. She saw and spoke to the power of our connection.
She communicated things to me I will never forget, things
that my soul recognized, things that hit me so viscerally my
entire body responded, not just my mind. She told me Roger
had been a warrior in another lifetime and had served to
protect. She told me that this was one of many lifetimes we
were together. As a warrior he said he would take a bullet
for me. In the physical world he would frequently say this
very expression to me and to his kids. She shared that this
was the last time our souls would ever have to face physical
separation. I felt this so, so deeply. This was one of the most
powerful experiences I've ever had because she pulled in so
much soul-level remembrance and recognition for me. With
awe and gratitude, I carry with me every day the truth that
she spoke during that interaction.

   After the grief retreat I was thankful to carry forward
new friends, new contacts, and new resources. One of those
resources was the Forever Family Radio show, which airs
weekly with a different a theme. One week listeners can call

in and share experiences, another they might talk about gifts and communication, and one of the four monthly shows offers an opportunity to call in and have a mini reading with the featured medium of the month.

For more than a month after the grief retreat, and I tried calling without getting through. The show is only an hour, so it goes by very fast with mini readings. One night I called and got placed on hold. The entire time I was on hold I was talking to Roger and writing to him how I really wanted a reading and for us to connect that night. Joe was hosting the show and the featured medium, Renee, had beautiful energy; there was a synchronicity with her background and us. I knew we were approaching the final reading of the night. I wrote down on a piece of paper: "Babe please push for us to get a turn before it's over." Renee was still reading the person before me and Joe was not doing readings; he had not contributed to a single reading all night. All of a sudden, Joe broke into Renee's reading: "I'm sorry to interrupt, but I have a man here pushing me, really pushing me to recognize his presence. Do you have a husband on the other side?" The woman who was getting the reading said no. You could tell Joe was frustrated because this husband was tap, tap, tapping on his shoulder. The reading ended and I got picked (of course, thank you Roger). Renee started and tied back amazing things, including Roger and I writing this book. She brought up how when I write the stories often of my hand cannot keep up because I'm channeling; he is writing with and through me. All of a sudden Joe said: "Did you happen to hear the end of the last caller?" I laughed and said yes and told him I had asked my Roger to push, push, push to get me on. He laughed and said: "Oh he did. He was making sure you got on before the show ended and you are the last reading of the night!" Joe said: "I kept hearing his name. Is his name RO something?" Indeed, Roger! Joe was so relieved. He knew it was settled and joked that otherwise Roger would be talking to him all night. I asked and I received, exactly how he heard me ask.

I want to end this chapter encouraging you to check out, join, and donate if you can, if you feel called, to the Forever Family Foundation. I know first-hand the work they do saves people. They are such a gift from above and are such an amazing resource for those grieving.

Reminders

REMINDERS COME IN MANY FORMS AND SYNCHRONICITIES. I HAVE heard multiple mediums say when we have a "random" thought (side note: I don't think anything is random anymore) of our person on the other side or suddenly visualize an experience of something we did with them, it is actually our person sending/ sharing that memory or experience our way. I love this and it certainly resonates with me. There are deep layers with these reminders.

One element that's been consistent throughout my reminders is presence. I have had several mediums tell me that my husband is here from the other side to lift me up like he did when he was here physically. They have said he wants me to always have abundance, to have nice things, which is consistent with how he was here. I definitely have felt his push to get the nicer things in life. We always joked about that here in the physical world, so it makes sense it would continue to come up and come through since he's crossed.

One such reminder with these types of layers was particularly poignant in a dream visit I had with Roger in late August. In this visit Roger and I had been traveling with our dog Mateo. My friend Diana appeared briefly in the dream; I wondered where she was, if she was with Roger. We continued on our trip and when we arrived at the hotel, Roger's suitcase was there, but he was not. He had left his cologne in his dopp kit with me. He wore a specific cologne, well it was actually an aftershave balm. It's a wonderful scent — one I don't know anyone else who wears — yet occasionally when I'm home or somewhere alone, I will suddenly catch the scent in the air and there is always a deep recognition that he is with me. I knew within the dream and immediately once I was awake that his message was that he is always with me. Even if I don't see him, his bags are there because he is there, no matter what.

The Mountains

THE SUMMER AFTER ROGER PASSED, I KNEW I WANTED, NEEDED, felt called to do our annual hike. I needed to represent the special tradition we had. Our hikes were epic and they tied back to so many gorgeous experiences, monumental life happenings for us. But I felt this trip had to look different. I knew it needed to be new enough so it would be healing, yet classic enough to be nostalgic. It couldn't be Rocky Mountain National Park or Jackson Hole or the Tetons or the Grand Canyon. So where? And with whom? It takes a special type of friend to be willing and able to commit to the intense level hikes Roger and I did. My friend Amber stepped up big. She knew how important this was for me, and she helped me heal on that trip more than she will ever fully realize.

We decided on Olympic National Park. It was perfect — west, but with a lush rainforest vibe that was so different from the Rockies or Wyoming. We got in late, technically next day, landing at SeaTac around 1:00 a.m. I got my first sign as soon as we arrived, on the jet bridge, before we even got to the gate. As I stepped off the plane pulling my rollaboard, I looked up to a man directly in front of me who had an iPad that read "Roger." I got chills, literally chills. We also experienced many angel numbers throughout the trip. I brought my Oracle deck and Amber wanted to pull cards on the second night. I pulled three cards for her and one for me. When I pulled mine, I asked in my mind about Roger's presence on our hikes. My card was "Beyond the Ordinary," which is all about spirit and spirit being present with us.

That night I had two dream visits in a row from Roger, which was rare while traveling. Both were different representations of us spending time with others then coming back to our favorite time of just us. I was so thankful to have these wonderful visits while traveling and recreating "our" trip.

The next day Amber and I went on a particularly difficult hike. We saw only six people the entire time, and only one was doing the full distance and elevation we were the rest stopped at the halfway point. We were at very high elevation and there were very few bugs, none after the halfway point. Amber was behind me. She had been taking photos, but for some reason (definitely called) she had switched to video. We were navigating really challenging terrain, with many downed trees. A very steep cliff off to our left made it a strategic effort to get over the trees. Most of the trees were so enormous we had to crawl, climb, scale, and scrape our way past and over them. We had just made it over a large section of downed trees and were going through a wetter section with smaller downed foliage. All of a sudden, a huge monarch butterfly flew inches from me, circled us and flew off, as a baby monarch started flying underneath it. I yelled with excitement and Amber caught the entire thing on video without even knowing it. We both had chills and just kept saying how amazing it was. We saw no other flying or non-flying insects the rest of the hike. We were still in awe when got to the top and saw our monarch friends. We talked about the amazing sign from Roger while we ate lunch, and Amber said: "What if he sends one for the way down?" I just smiled and laughed. In my head I said: "Babe, can you show us one on the way down?"

About a third of the way down, a huge hawk flew out around where we were hiking. It was hidden in a nest in the mountain, but we hadn't seen it on the way up. Two very clear and magical signs — monarchs and hawks are regular signs from Roger.

The hike was absolutely breathtaking. I'm not at all surprised Roger let us know he was with us, as it oozed everything he would have loved: challenging terrain, no people, gorgeous views, and an enchanted vibe — totally our type of hike. As we completed the final mile or so, Amber and I both looked up and gasped as beautiful monarch flew around us. She said: "My comment at the top of the mountain — he did it!" I told her, even better I had asked him to send us one more monarch on the way down in my head. We were both full of body chills. Magic.

The night I returned from the trip I had another dream visit. The next morning, first thing, when I opened the front door for my early morning walk, a huge monarch greeted me.

Roger is always with me. He is my protector and cheerleader. We love each other endlessly across dimensions. That is our gift to ourselves and each other.

Fairways and Raptors

As I've mentioned, Roger was beyond passionate about the game of golf. He included Mateo in our putting contests, with Roger putting between Mateo's front paws. It was a game he and Roger loved.

I knew the basics of the game having worked at a golf course in high school and college, but Roger taught me to play. He had a beautiful swing and was a scratch player who always downplayed his enormous skill set. He was also an awesome teacher. Over the years, many friends and family called to tell him an issue they were having with their game and he always knew how to fix it. They often sent him a video of their swing and he came to the rescue. With some, he knew their game so well he automatically knew old patterns that needed adjustment.

Roger was the perfect teacher for me. Being a competitive perfectionist, I had what I am sure were very unreasonable expectations of myself when I started really playing. He always knew exactly when to say something and when to hold back. He helped my swing and also helped club me, identify the perfect club to hit based on the distance and my length to hit each club, I learned, and the way he did it really helped build my confidence. There was comfort in playing with him; he was the person I played with most. His son Jeff joined us frequently before he moved and whenever he was in town, but often it was just Roger and I. He knew this was how I liked it, how I was most comfortable, as opposed to playing with strangers. I know he preferred it as well. Frequently, twosomes get paired with other people, especially on weekends, which was largely when we played. Roger had all these extremely effective hacks to ensure it was just us. It didn't hurt that many people in the industry knew him, so the pros did him frequent favors. The only time we regularly played with other people was when we were traveling. If we were on a personal trip, we frequently tried to work in a little golf. Sometimes on work trips we went out a little early or stayed for a weekend to get in a round.

Once Roger became ill, neither of us played. I honestly never even thought of it. There were so many more important things.

When Roger was in hospice, he told me multiple times he wanted me to play golf. He didn't want me to quit the game. He also told his son Jeff, he wanted me to keep playing. Playing again was going to be very emotional and challenging for me. I'm very thankful Jeff played with me the first two times out. I'm not sure he even realized that he did so many little things Roger always did for me while playing golf, which made me confident and comfortable.

I only played about half a dozen times the summer and fall after Roger crossed over, but that's about half a dozen more than I would have predicted. Every time I played, I had signs from Roger. Those signs definitely motivated me to play. The course I played was close to home and was particularly gorgeous and wooded. One round in particular in early fall I saw and was circled by monarchs more than a dozen times. I saw butterflies on almost every hole. Towards the end of the round, I walked up the middle of the fairway and felt a compelling need to look above me. I had just hit my second shot following a very nice tee ball. I had hit my hybrid, a go to for me, and it was a good hit. I looked up to see a huge hawk flying directly above me. He circled me before flying off. That was total confirmation for me from Roger, and I was filled with joy and gratitude.

Roger's son Jeff organized a memorial golf tournament. The signs at that tournament were so strong. Right after I hit the drive that ended up winning the longest drive competition for the event, my phone lit up flashing 11:11. On the 18th hole, I looked up and a hawk was right above me as I completed the round right before it started to rain. Roger's round, totally for you baby!

Phone Calls and Magic

TWO DAYS AFTER ROGER'S MEMORIAL GOLF TOURNAMENT I RECEIVED a call from Bill, the head of operations at the course. I'd left him a message to thank him for all the amazing things they did to help us honor Roger. They were outstanding and flexible as we worked our way through the details of the first memorial tournament. I mentioned that I had won the longest drive competition, and that I really hadn't expected it. I was too caught up in the drive and 11:11, in feeling Roger with me especially on that hole particularly, that I didn't think to take a photo of the sign in the fairway listing my 'ame first. The director of operations immediately offered to recreate the sign and take a photo for me. I was thrilled, since it meant so much to me at the first anniversary event to have my name directly below Roger's. I knew it would be a beautiful keepsake.

Bill apologized for the fact that he was calling from the car, but said he was on his way to play a very special round of golf. He mentioned he hadn't been getting out to play much that season and he was sneaking out to play a prestigious, phenomenal course in the area. Roger had talked about all the special spots nearby and he had played most of them many times. Bill told me he was playing at Rich Harvest Farms. Of all the people in our golf network, Roger is the only person I ever heard talk about Rich Harvest Farms. He had been invited to play there a few times and absolutely raved about how pretty and challenging the course was, and how well-groomed it was. He also talked about an antique car museum on the property and detailed all the cars, showing me great photos from the course and the museum. I was taken back by the mention of the course and felt Roger's presence in the conversation. The director and I talked about Roger's memorial tournament and one of his favorite courses, as well as my golf game. I say that with humility, but Roger was so proud of my play and would have loved that winning drive, especially since he taught me.

This great conversation it was early in the morning, so I jumped in the shower to get ready for work after the call. While I was in the shower, my phone rang several times. I thought maybe Bill from the course had forgotten to tell me something about the memorial. As I hopped out of the shower, I checked my phone just as it was on the final ring. The calls were from Roger's cell phone. I smiled, laughed, cried, and had chills, in total awe and amazement yet again. There are no limits to love. There are no limits to the magic we can receive. Open your mind, your heart, and your soul to receive all the magic, joy, and blessings they can bring for us.

Throughout the rest of that day, photos of monarchs and frogs showed up on my phone — just more validation that left me feeling so wonderfully loved.

Memorial Golf

EACH OF THE TWO YEARS THAT HAVE NOW PASSED SINCE ROGER transitioned, we have had a memorial golf tournament in his honor. As I previously mentioned at the first one, I was so proud, because I knew he was behind it, I won the longest drive. Both years there were so many signs and messages the day of the tournament. Because Roger was really *the* person I played golf with and I have played only a handful of times since he passed, I get anxious when I am going to play. There are a lot of elements that give me anxiety, the largest one is that golf was what we did most weekends as a couple and golf was such a big thing for Roger. Second, having played competitive sports and being a bit of a perfectionist, I have expectations of myself, I have always put pressure on myself with my play but it's worse now that I feel I am in some ways representing us and add on top of that the fact I don't play with any consistency, all factors lead to me being anxious for a round. I had not played all summer and then Jeff and I started talking about planning for the 2nd memorial I thought wow I have to get out. First, I went and hit balls twice, that went well, and I had even been anxious about that since it was a new course in a new town. Having that under my belt helped though. I then had an opportunity with a private women's executive group I am in to play at a really nice private club and get in a full round. I was really happy with my round; I had a few times and areas of struggle but overall considering it had been about 10 months since I played it was a big success. Next, I snuck out and walked 9 at a public course by me. There were lots of signs, primarily in the form of interventions, when I played the 9 alone. Roger and I always liked to play fast, I play really fast. I play so fast that often someone will talk, take out a club, or move a cart in my back swing because they had no idea, I was about to hit that quickly. Roger loved this about me. As you know from previous chapters plus my references of anxiety in this one, I prefer to not play with strangers. Stranger danger ☺. Now the public course I went to is always busy, I mean always, even when it is super-hot or raining and on weekdays. There are always people waiting to hit. I drive by the course frequently and I am always shocked how busy it is. This is the same course I went to in order to hit balls, both times super busy. So, I go out, I drive up, head in to the shop to pay. I was going to walk 9 during a workday around lunch time. It was August but there was beautiful breeze as soon as I got to the course. They let me walk no problem, they showed me what hole to start on, they said nothing about playing with anyone else. I am in disbelief as I walk to the first hole. But I get there and long behold there is no one they are pairing me with. So, I quickly tee off, this is the point I realize there is no one in front of me. I was hitting it great. Driving the ball really well, so was smiling (up) at Roger the entire time. I played 9, walking on a relatively hilly course, in 1.5 hours… super-fast. I played completely alone with the exception of catching up to a guy who told me to hit and play through. Now I am telling this next part in no way at all to brag but knowing full well Roger was behind the power in my swing. I get up to the hole, there is a guy and his girlfriend, she is not playing she is just watching, and he is without a doubt trying to show boat. I had been watching them for a few holes since I was catching up and you could tell he was trying to really be full of himself to impress her. So I step up, he motions for me to hit. He had already tee'd off and his ball was in the fairway. I step up and drive my ball at least a third further than him, he has a look of total shock. I walk up and hit my 2nd shot on the green and immediately was surrounded by butterflies. If I had scripted the perfect 9 I would not have done as good of a job as my hubby on the other side, absolute perfection!

That was the last time I played before the 2nd memorial. Now at the first memorial I was partnered up with two gentlemen who grew up with Roger in Des Moines. They knew each other's families and they are both investors in our company. One is a prominent attorney, Beau, and the other a retired judge, Art. Their energy and vibe are so in line with Roger's. Beau has been a huge God send with all things related to the business, particularly in times where my first thought is I need Roger, somehow each time Beau would magically step in without me even asking and carry the weight. They are both very good players and played competitively when they were young. The first year it was the 3 of us teeing off together, we were the first group. Playing with them was perfect. They would help me track my ball and we had such a great time. They made it fun when it could have been a bit anxiety filled for me. The 2nd year we were scheduled to play together as a group again and the first group to tee off but were supposed to have a 4th and his wife join us. I have to admit was secretly worried about the change in dynamic just since we had such a great trio the first year. Well, we get up to the first hole and wait and they did not show up so it was our trio again. Over the course of the beautiful, fun memorial round I had so many signs. Walking up to the first hole a hawk flew right over me, so close I could have touched him. Out of the 3 9-hole courses we could have been sent to the second 9 we played had an enormous flower garden shaped like you guessed it a butterfly, and "out of nowhere" the guys asked if they could take my picture with it in the background. I had been thinking the entire walk up to the green I was going to ask them without sounding weird, no need! Then literally on the next hole, while stating the yardage Beau says 527 two times in a row, I just started laughing, that is Roger's birthday. I had a monarch fly around me a few holes later. And we had an eagle follow above us for two holes. As we were coming off 18 finishing up, we were walking over this pretty bridge and a favorite Frank Sinatra song, Summer Wind, starts playing from the club house as a group of monarchs circle me on the bridge. As if that were not perfect enough, I was talking to our board Chair a few days later as he asked how the memorial went. I told him the stories and how perfect it was, and I mentioned how it was great we had our trio for the 2nd year in a row, he goes oh Lindsay you had a *foursome* both years! Of course!!! That huge sign was right there, and it all clicked when he said that. So perfect.

Giving Thanks

THE FIRST THANKSGIVING AFTER ROGER PASSED WAS A BLUR. I WAS like a zombie or robot, just going through the motions. My body was moving but almost on autopilot. Year two, as I was driving to Mary's family home, the same place I had gone the year before, I had flashbacks of parts of the drive from my comatose state the first year. Going to my friend's was the right choice for me; it was different and there were no expectations of me, except to make a few fresh pies. I could arrive when I wanted and leave when I wanted, so if I got too overwhelmed or sad or even just exhausted, I could call it completely on my terms. This is exactly what I needed.

I talked to Roger the entire drive about the difference in the two years. I thanked him for his beautiful strong presence, for all he brought in for me every day. I thanked him for our phenomenal partnership. I asked him to show me a sign that he was going to Thanksgiving dinner with me that night. I had done the exact same drive the year before, past the same restaurants, stores, and streets; past the same houses and corners, and probably most of the same Christmas decorations and lights. Not even five minutes after asking Roger for validation that he was with me, I drove past a house lit to the nines, Christmas decor on every inch of the lawn. This was not your standard Christmas fare; this house was decorated in all froggy themed Christmas decor, including a giant frog dressed in Christmas apparel and lit up in the middle of the front lawn.

A few days later I was outside early in the morning, talking to Mary again. I told her my plans to celebrate Christmas with the kids. Roger's son Jeff was coming into town, so he, Meghan, her new husband, and I were all going to have dinner. I told Mary how I was going to do our unique holiday tradition of a seafood extravaganza. I told her how excited we all were, but also lamented a little about how crazy the price of shellfish had gotten. Right as I was saying how it was three to four times higher than any other year, a huge red tail hawk flew right through us. Just to make sure we noticed, the hawk did this crazy sideways dive through the bushes and went out the other side right next to us. He looked like one of those trick fighter planes in an air show. We were both in total awe and it was so fitting, not only regarding Roger wanting us to be together celebrating Christmas as a family, but also as another reminder he did not want me stressing and counting pennies.

Holidays

GIVEN THE AMAZING GIFT ROGER SENT AND THE EXTRAORDINARY way he delivered it the first Christmas after he transitioned, I wondered how things would play out the second Christmas. Well, he had special surprises in store for me year two as well. The first gift I received arrived by FedEx. It was a box of delicious gourmet truffle chocolates, super high end. I did not order them and had never heard of the company that sent them. They were addressed to me with a special card and arrived a day after my initial thoughts of what Roger might have in store for this Christmas.

Gifts two and three happened on a Sunday morning when one of my closest friends, Mary, asked me to go to a flea market with her. I was reluctant to go because I had planned to work out and I am not really a flea market person. Though Mary is not a flea market person either, she really wanted to go see a friend of hers with a high-end jewelry shop and a table at the show. This friend has tons of gorgeous jewelry, beautiful and unique pieces. Roger had gotten me gifts from her, stunning pieces. I told Mary that as long as I could stay in my workout gear, I was in. We walked through row after row. Mary stopped to look at a table and I went to the next shop, where I immediately saw a beautiful, never touched, super feminine tablecloth – Roger loved feminine things for me. As I opened it, I saw the pretty embroidery with butterflies on the corners — it was only five dollars (almost free).

We made our way to the station with her friend's great jewelry. There were already several people asking to see her pieces. I looked around her display cases. A few weeks prior, a medium told me how Roger wanted me to have all the nice things and not to ever worry about lack. He said if I wanted something, I should get it. I tried on a pretty enamel ring from an Italian artist, a designer Roger had gotten me a gorgeous bracelet from previously. The bracelet I have from this designer is gorgeous pink and white enamel with pink sapphires inlaid in a feminine floral pattern. I went to the main case and tried on a bunch of pretty rings and the jeweler started talking to us. She mentioned Roger of Roger and Holland jewelry at least five times. She kept saying Roger this, Roger that. The entire time I smiled to my core just knowing. My friend bought a few things and as she was checking out, I tried on the enamel ring one more time. As I slipped it back into the case, Mary asked how much the ring cost. The jeweler asked if it was for me. When Mary said yes, the jeweler said: "She can have it." Then she turned to me and said: "It's yours Lindsay take it!" Thank you baby. Merry Christmas!

Merging Worlds

I HAVE NOTICED AN AMAZING FLOW AND BLENDING, ENERGY AND love with messaging between my waking and dream states. Many times, elements in the waking world are addressed in our dream visits. This is especially the case with critical messaging of Roger's return, his wellness, and his presence with me. One night a few days following the Christmas dinner hawk sign, I had a dream visit where Roger and I were discussing the signs he sent me before he came back. I talked to him about the amazing way he used hawks to communicate with me. Specifically, I talked to him about the hawk during my conversation about Christmas dinner with the kids.

This is one example, but I have consistently seen the connection and crossover, that blend and merging as we have built and strengthened our communication systems. Another powerful example came in a dream visit where we had in-depth discussion about our entire way of communicating now that he was on the other side. In this visit, he was back and so we talked about when we were physically separated, the ways we had been able to stay so intimately connected. I asked if he remembered how his higher self and my higher self were able to stay connected after he crossed over, that we communicated through our higher selves. He started sobbing, remembering the emotions of all we had done to keep our partnership growing in love. It was so powerful, I felt it so deeply in and out of the dream visit. I knew it was our truth.

My pre-bed routine is always to talk to Roger and invite him to visit me. On this particular night I had asked that we see each other and show each other our future love together. After the visit and conversation about our higher selves, I got up and journaled the conversation and went back to bed. As soon as I fell back asleep, he greeted me and asked if that made me happy. And I answered: "Yes, thank you!"

Season's Greetings

DURING THE HOLIDAY SEASON OF THE SECOND YEAR THERE WERE many synchronicities, signs, and visits. I received quite a few additional gifts from Roger. In the evening I love to do a pre-bed stroll around the block. It helps center me, ground me with oneness, nature, and energy. It is also a perfect, totally silent time for me to talk to Roger, often telling him my gratitude for what he helped bring in for me that day.

A week before Christmas, on my evening walk, the night was perfect a cool, crisp 30 degrees, the sky totally clear. That's my favorite, when I can see the moon and stars shining especially bright over the golf course that Roger loved. Suddenly, the most stunning shooting star came down right in front of me, dropping as it went sideways. It was totally amazing. I have seen so few shooting stars. On many of our trips out west, we would lay out at night watching for them. Roger saw them much more often than I did. I saw a few in Africa years ago, but not many here in the States.

Meghan and I had been talking about them a few days earlier. She had been out west for her honeymoon, her first trip to Jackson Hole. She had asked Roger to send her a shooting star because her new hubby, Craig, had seen several on the trip. That night in the early morning hours she saw several. I told her I had only ever seen a few. I remember thinking the next night how it would be really cool to see one, and I said: "What do you think Babe, can you send one?" And the most amazing one dropped across my path. I have never seen one move like this one.

On the Move

FOR MONTHS I HAD BEEN GETTING SIGNS, MESSAGES, AND NUGGETS from Roger about a move in my future, certainly not something my human brain would have come up with. I loved my neighborhood. Most of my friends and family are local. I have been in the Chicago burbs my entire adult life and have developed a good, safe, comfortable system of operating. But I trusted the signs and listened right away about the move.

My destination seems to be a beacon Roger is calling me to for the next phase in our journey. I knew and saw the connection he and my guides were making with this new spot and the work I'm being called to do. I know this new city will be part of the puzzle for my healing journey, not only healing me or us, but helping others as well. I have this knowing and trust that this is the why behind this unbelievable pain and grief; it is related to our larger purpose as souls together. We are able to work collectively with him on the other side, guiding me with my total trust in the process, not knowing the how, but understanding that it relates to our purpose and our amazing bond. Our gorgeous partnership is taking on new meaning and form. We have been gifted this phenomenal relationship, and in return our gift is to use what we've learned and bring it to others to help them.

I've been guided to move to Tennessee. I believe we will be starting a community, a system, a retreat to support people in deep grief. We are being called to build this, deliver it in a way that has never been done before. At the end of 2021, I went to visit Tennessee. This is how my mom and I brought in the new year. Since I was really carried, called to take this new journey, I received some amazing signs and validations on the trip. We looked at several potential areas to live. I had a knowing before seeing anything that this one specific town was the place. In my gut, I knew it was the one. We dedicated three days to looking at three towns to get a feel for the areas and the housing. The second day, the day we were looking at the town I had a feeling about, my rental car was repeatedly circled and followed by hawks for the entire five hours we toured. It was mind blowing; we had two to four hawks above us almost constantly the entire day. During the trip I repeatedly saw 11:11 on clocks everywhere.

One of the first nights after Roger passed, I had a dream visit of us at our house. He was recovering and getting strong. We talked about getting a new house and even about moving to Tennessee but decided not to worry about it until he was ready. We did decide to start preparing and getting the house ready to sell. Our little yorkie Maddy was with us in the visit. This dream visit helped pave the way for the trip with my mom and validated it was the right move; it also led the way to other signs.

In addition to seeing 11:11 on clocks, my phone, and online, there was one sign that really stood out. While looking at one of the neighborhoods on the final day before flying back to Chicago, we saw a car parked in a weird spot, so much so that it stood out. It was in a brand-new development and no one really lived there yet. It was New Year's Day so not many people were out and about, plus the weather was questionable, super windy and rainy off and on. I commented on the "randomly" parked car and then noticed the license plate: 1111 JOY. "Hi Baby, glad you could help!"

Been Here All Day

ONE DAY IN JANUARY MY GRIEF WAS MORE CHALLENGING; I WAS getting caught up in old patterns, focusing on the physical loss, and feeling very much like I needed a visit. It had been about a week since our last visitation dream. I had plenty of angel numbers and signs over those days but was stuck focusing on loss. My grief comes in waves and sometimes I have no idea what triggers my mind to go down that path of sadness and crying.

Crying and sadness are so healing and healthy. It helps us move with and through the grief, the loss of our physical bond, but if we don't let it move through us, it can take us down to a rabbit hole. I recall feeling very much like I needed to see him that day, so going into my pre-bed routine, I was particularly emotional asking for a visit.

I woke up off and on a few times throughout the night. In the deep of the night, probably around 4:00 a.m., I had a visit. I was with my parents and brother. We were out and about, and when we returned to our house, I thought it was just the four of us. I walked from the kitchen, where I had been talking to my parents, and saw Roger laying on the couch. I was so, so happy. It was as if within the dream I recognized my need ˙om outside of the dream to see Roger. In a very excited voice

I said: "I didn't know you were here, honey, I'm so happy!" He responded: "I've been here the whole time!" It was a clear message: stop fretting, I'm always with you. Later in the visit he kissed me right before I woke up; after he kissed me, he again asked: "Did that make you happy? Is that what you wanted?" I said yes. It was exactly what I asked for, exactly what I needed, and such a beautiful reminder.

Springtime: The Move

SOMETIMES WHEN YOUR LOVED ONE(S), SPIRIT OR GOD ARE HELPING you see the highest path your signs come in the form of total easy and so many synchronicities. My move and literally element of the move feel into this category. When I started getting the whispers, nudges, dreams and other visualizes about the idea of me moving I honestly had no intention at all of moving. Not moving homes, not moving locations, and certainly not moving to another state. The last time I lived in another state I was a child under my parents' care. I have never moved to another state as an adult, which was probably a good thing for spirit because I went in not knowing how much more was involved than moving locally. So, as I was getting the whispers I was open, I was listening. I did anticipate divine timing of the move to be slower, pace, ease because it was slow. So not the case at all. I remember telling my dad with an absolute, truly heart felt undertone that it was not at all immanent. I actually thought it would be a few years. Part of the signs I was getting were about a new house, brand new construction. So, I thought oh I will work with a builder. Pick a house plan or have an architect create one and build a new house. I couldn't imagine this being less than two years out. I started looking at towns online, researching areas, I had always loved the vibe of Nashville. I had been there a few times for work, the people were so nice and the city just had a great feel and flow. I had never once considered living there but just enjoyed it. When I started researching and looked at probably 6 or so towns, there was one that as soon as I saw it I knew. I didn't say anything to anyone, I kept it to myself, but it was definitely an intuitive hit, this was it. When my mom and I came to look at 4 towns, Nashville proper being one, I did not say anything about the hit. The more we drove around, ruled out areas and looked at houses it became very obvious the intuitive hit was 100% accurate and that was the town we ended up in. Our goal with that trip was really to pick an area, not make an offer or buy anything just land on the area we thought would be best. In a perfect world, best best-case scenario we loved the idea of being walkable to each other's houses, maybe a mile or less away. The market in Nashville in particular was and is insane. Take the rest of the US in 2022 with the housing market explosion and put it on major steroids, that was Nashville. People I knew here and people I knew from out of state wanting to move to Nashville were telling me story after story of putting offers on 30-40 houses, $20-$100k over ask with no contingencies and losing it to another buyer. Our realtor was preparing us about that. Lots were impossible to get, builders were not taking custom projects, they didn't need to they could build to their specs and sell to hundreds of competing buyers with no questions asked.

I had found a builder and an architect I really loved early on. My mom was going more the direction of existing home. We had thought she would be moved and established while I was likely building, and it would be slower and more gradual for me. Before we had even started talking about the move or before I started looking at towns I would have "random" emails about moving to TN, I received a post card in the mail about buying land outside Nashville. People would "randomly" mention Nashville or someone they knew who lived there and loved it. I was getting signs left and right. When I did start looking, I had a huge one. Weeks after looking at builders online and looking at their floor plans, I was showing Mary the one I was having the instinct about. I was on their site, I had been on it multiple times before, and all the sudden I clicked a floor plan that had everything I wanted, and specks that are not at all common here. It literally checked all the boxes, I look as I was showing her, the name of the plan "The Stanton." I was literally beaming. Over the course of the few months that followed I had so many signs including from mediums as well as every other form of sign.

Once we found the town and committed to move things happened so fast and with such ease. The market was hot in Chicago, not anything like Nashville but I thought I would see. Worse case I would rent while building. While I was deciding, I had the contract to list with my realtors but was on the fence about committing, we all the sudden find out that builder I (we) loved had a brand new, rather private development he was building in THE town I was being pulled to. My mom had just listed her house and the first weekend had two above ask offers from strong buyers wanting to move to Phoenix. We found out "off the record" the builder was going to be listing a few houses that were near completion. They would list on a Friday, and you had till Monday morning to give your highest and best, they do not take escalation clauses (where the bid automatically raises for you if others bid above your initial offer). And the build was not taking any contingent offers. My mom submitted a health, above ask offer on the house she likes best of the two, she had a continency. There were multiple offers, yet she won the house!! We had no idea how many, we knew it was very limited, houses the builder was going to build and sell and we had no idea the timing. So, with that information and my mom set, I listed my house in IL. I had an intuitive hit on a very, I mean very specific list price. I also had a hit on the sell price (above ask). My realtors debated me on but trusted me, trusted my intuition. We listed at my price, after no showings only an open house we sold the house first week above ask at the exact price I had told them.

The buyers needed a fast close, I could potentially be homeless haha. But I trusted. Again, no idea if the builder would finish and list any houses in the two-week window, I absolutely had to find something. Not just because my house was selling but also because it was beyond difficult to hire a moving company. You had to book in advance. Literally the last weekend, against the wall for both a moving company commitment and a place to live, the builder released two homes. It's funny to me, I love the builder's style, but only one of the 20 or so houses in my neighborhood he built would I say also totally fit Roger's taste as well. That is the house I bought, the house I won. It literally has everything Roger talked about in a house all the years we were together, it checks all my boxes and all of his. It is 4 houses away from my mothers. Brand new construction, exactly what I would have built but without the wait time. I put my offer in on Saturday, and they had until Monday at noon to tell me if I won or not. At 11:59 my friend Ann Marie, the neighbor with Roger's playlist on her pandora who always talks to me about signs and communications, got in her car and as soon as she did REO Speedwagon, "Time for me to Fly" came on. That is one of Roger's signs, a song he played for us that night she and I were talking about all of his signs, a song he played for me constantly when dating, and a most fitting song for my move. Right after I got the call the house was mine. She told me as soon as that song came on she knew.

SECTION 3

How-to Guide to Connection

Tune In

OUR LOVED ONES ON THE OTHER SIDE USE ENERGY TO COMMUNICATE. In this third and final section I want to provide a user guide of sorts, the steps you will need to help you connect and recognize when your loved one is sending you messages and gifts from other side.

I will start with a perfect example of tuning in. Around the holidays of year two mark, I was having a day of self-doubt and letting my egoic mind creep in, not horribly, but enough to sit over top of the day like a dark cloud. I was stressed about work and wanting to see revenue faster. I had been working to expand an already large customer of ours. We had put a huge proposal in front of them several weeks prior. Over the preceding several months, we had achieved very nice incremental growth from this customer, but no bite yet on the full enchilada. I was letting doubt creep in and create stress and worry about money.

Roger has clearly, and in multiple ways, communicated with me about not concerning myself with thoughts of potential lack. He has assured me, and come through with a few straight up miracles, that I will not be in a position of doing without. But I still let my thoughts snowball. In retrospect, I'm sure the emotions of the impending holidays were a factor as well. We all face doubt and can head down rabbit holes.

I had sent the client an email about the proposal the week before and was due to send another check in on this specific day. I drafted a simple follow up email before heading to a dentist appointment. Roger was a straight up celebrity at our dentist office; they adored him. The receptionist lost her spouse when she was around my age and we always have deep conversations when I visit. She is a very spiritual person, as is my dentist, who lost his teenage son in a boating accident. He recognizes and receives signs from his son regularly. The energy at the office is very tuned in and receptive.

Between X rays, I was listening to the standard bad Christmas music they piped through the speakers throughout the office — classic Christmas carols one right after another. The technician stepped out to get the dentist and I was by myself in deep thought. Suddenly, this song came on that did not fit at all; not Christmas whatsoever and the lyric repeated over and over again: "don't worry baby, don't worry baby" with the final line "everything will turn out alright." I had practically been in tears right before that song came on, lying there worrying. I knew that song was for me, a clear message and reminder. It stood out so starkly against every other song that had played.

I went home and reread my draft email to the client, checking for typos. I was about to hit send when something inside me told me not to send this generic follow up. If you want a different result, do something different. The messaging told me to lay everything out for them, show them how it would work, and that all they had to do was say yes. I completely re-crafted the message and ended the email with "all we need is a yes." Ten minutes later I got my yes. We doubled our business with this large client. So many elements that I received that day came together. I started with knowing that the song was out of place, recognizing that it stood out. I recognized it was a clear message for me. That allowed me to tune in fully and listen to all the important help and guidance Roger provided.

Tools

In this section I want to dive into the tools I have found invaluable in helping me connect. I will cover what has worked for me in an effort to assist you, and let you know from my perspective the non-negotiables and the ones I consider icing on your beautiful connection cake. After reviewing each tool and how I have personally seen it work, I will provide a sample day so you have the tools as well as the flow I have found particularly helpful.

Meditation

Regardless of what level of experience you have with meditation, this tool is absolutely one of my non negotiables. I have made meditation part of my daily routine no matter what. There is so much amazing data and research on the value and tremendous impact a meditation practice has on all aspects of life. I was initially drawn to meditation or, as I now believe, guided to it to help me sleep. When I was so deep in grief, it was a way to calm my mind and my nervous system. I lay in bed thinking, trying to solve problems, replaying things, wanting the thoughts to stop, but with no idea how to make that happen. Once I started meditating after Roger passed, I have had the most consistent deep sleep of my life.

Why does this matter for connection? When you are in your deepest sleep, you are most likely to have a visitation dream. This is why research shows, and my own experience has been pretty consistent, you are most likely to have a dream visit between 2:00 and 4:00 a.m. To connect, just like to sleep well, you have to shut your mind off from "human thoughts," tune out, and get rid of the minutiae. You need to release the details or challenges from the day that bog your focus. To really be able to open up and receive, you need to let these distractions go. Strong sleep patterns and a consistent sleep routine keeps you mentally healthier in the day. You are less likely to get overwhelmed or extremely anxious in your grief if you are rested. I know I require more sleep now as a result of grief and I honor that. I listen to my body and do not skip sleep. I notice a major deterioration in my overall mental health related to grief if I do not listen to my needs. Healthy sleep is so important to releasing the day and its stress. Meditation is an unbelievably effective way to do that.

Meditation does not need to be long to be effective. The longest meditations I do are 25 to 30 minutes. The ones I do nightly are typically only three to five minutes. Commit to a practice that works for you on every level. If you find it takes you a little longer to get in a relaxed and open state, then set that time aside. The longer you commit to the practice and make it your daily routine, the easier you will flow into an open meditative state. Don't get frustrated just sitting in silence if that is all you can do at first. Trust me, this is progress. Even if thoughts or distractions come in, let them float through. See them and let them pass by. Being still opens you and the pathway to connect. If you are new to a meditation practice or just find it challenging, I recommend a chanting meditation, which is how I started and I still do nightly.

Many people have told me they struggle to shut their head off and get frustrated trying to meditate. I always suggest chanting meditation. They return to me happy and thankful it worked. Why does it work? Chanting gives you another area of focus; your mind can't run wild with thoughts from the day if you're focused on repeating a chant. I found a wonderful three-minute meditation chant I do every night before bed (see the resource guide). Even if I'm traveling and get in very late, I do my three-minute meditation before bed. Trust me, it's worth it. There are great apps you can use to help you to do a guided meditation or even if you just want relaxing music in the background. I have personally used the *Headspace* and *Simple Habit* apps, but there are many great ones available, as well great content online. If you want a peaceful background sound, try playing singing bowls in the background through online music streaming.

Visualizations

I love adding visualizations to the end of my meditation practice, particularly before bed. I find it helps me connect and seems to really open me up for a visitation dream. I do my three to ten minutes of nightly meditation then take five to ten minutes to do a visualization. I like to set a timer on my phone, partially because it helps me make sure I get to bed on time to get my eight hours of sleep. Keeping a tight, consistent schedule around your sleeping routine will help you tremendously. It helps your body know when to go into those deep, deep, sleep patterns.

For me, visualization started relatively simply and has grown. It is still pretty simple, but I have expanded my options. When I first started, and what I suggest to beginners, is to pick a few places that you'd like to go, to take yourself. I picked two places I wanted to be, two places that deeply resonated for me and for us, places I could see in my mind's eye, places I could see Roger and I enjoying. We went to these two places in the physical world, and that just felt right for my visualizations. Both of mine connect with nature and are really beautiful places where we were tuned into each other. When I visualize these places, it is one hundred percent about us — our energy, our love, our soul connection — so it's easy to put myself there. It feels amazing. If you pick a place you went to in the physical world, you may want to look at a photo of yourself and your loved one there before doing the visualization. This can really help you get there with ease.

I set my timer and I go deep into our world for that five minutes. I visualize the things we did or what I wanted us to do in that moment. I visualize and really feel our love. I smell the smell of his aftershave. I feel the texture of his hands on mine. I fully immerse myself in the memory and experience. Immersing yourself in memory can help you go deep into the experience. Say what you want to say, see what you want to see and, most importantly, feel what you want to feel. Feel your love. Feel every detail — the sounds, smells, taste, and sights.

Visualization is an amazingly powerful tool. Combined with and following meditation it can really open you up for an amazing pathway. It can open the doors of connection in a magnificent way. I love doing this power packed duo right before bed because I've repeatedly experienced how it opens me up to receive Roger. This leads to wonderful and meaningful dream visits.

Gratitude

If you really want a profound way to open yourself to the other side, make it a trifecta: meditation followed by a short visualization and closing with a gratitude practice. This is what I do immediately before I fall asleep. You may even find you fall asleep in the middle of your gratitude practice. Again, this can be really short. Mine are 30 seconds to a minute long each night. As I lay in bed, I thank Roger for all of the gifts, blessings, and signs he has brought me that day.

I thank him for the deep relationship we have. I thank him for our forever soul connection. I thank him for guiding and watching over me each day. And I always tell him I'm open to receive him and any messaging he has for me that night; any nuggets of information he wants to share. It is particularly important, I have found, to be open to insights from your visits that are applicable to your life in the physical realm. In addition to the warmth, love, and comfort they bring, they can bring guidance to help you in the physical world. This can come in the form of a preview to help alleviate anxiety, or a piece of information or perspective on a situation you had not seen before. I frequently get outstanding insights, clarity, and perspective with visitations. Sometimes it's so powerful, a matter of him showing me something to give me a level of clarity that allows me to completely release attachment to outcomes here. This is something I normally would not be able to do, but it comes naturally and with beautiful ease when we have visits like this.

My gratitude practice extends beyond Roger. I first express my thanks to him, of course, but I follow with thanking God, the divine or source— whatever resonates most with you. It may depend on the day. I also thank my spirit team. I have been told by several mediums that Roger and I have a team behind us, helping show us the path, helping him guide me so we can collectively help others. I thank our spirit team, I thank my loved ones on the other side.

This is a wonderful opportunity to add in elements you want to manifest. Thank God, source, your loved ones, for all of the abundance and gifts they are bringing in. Thank them for assisting you in your spiritual journey. Thank them for helping you see your soul's purpose. Thank them for all of the love they are calling in for you. Even if there are areas where you are struggling, this can be a great opportunity to thank them for their guidance. It is an opportunity to call them in, invite them in, so they can help. Open that door to allow them to assist you. Gratitude is so powerful. It connects you with the highest vibration of energy. It connects you with love. Through this higher vibration, through this love, it helps open you up to receive more powerful communication. You may find you hear not only from your loved ones, but you may also get very strong, deep messaging from God / source and your angels. Again, I find meditation, visualization, and gratitude are a super powerful trio.

Journaling

Journaling is such an important part of my practice. I started journaling before Roger's transition to the other side. I journaled all our conversations and plans from those final weeks he was in hospice. I journaled our phone calls, the details around what we discussed, including timing and elements he mentioned when we were having deep conversations around staying connected after he passed. Because I wrote a lot of these experiences and conversations down, it was very natural for me to continue.

One cathartic thing I did after he passed was to collect all the notes I had made. Many times, I made notes on my phone once he fell asleep. I felt drawn to put this all in a handwritten journal. I had a very pretty metallic book I had never used that fit the bill perfectly. I wrote a day-by-day account of all of those notes and conversations. It was a beautiful experience, taking me to being there with him and feeling so much at peace in our conversations. Writing them made them feel even more purposeful, reinforcing the knowledge that these plans would happen, that he would be with me. He would come back and make it known to me that he was here with me. Journaling is so healing, both when you're writing and when you come back to read it. Writing my notes in a fancy journal was a wonderful connection.

As soon as I started getting signs, which was immediately (I had a large one moments after he passed), I wrote them down in the journal. I write the date, each angel number I see — usually as it happens so I don't forget — any signs or crazy awesome synchronicities, and of course, any dream visits. I try to track the time of dream visits as well. I keep the journal on my desk so it's easy to track angel numbers. I almost always have several throughout the day.

Journaling helps you track, record, and recall details. Journaling feels good. I have noticed that grief can lead to forgetfulness (kind of a fog), so tracking details is very important. It feels good to write what you're loved one is sending you. It's another form of gratitude. Your loved ones see that it's important to you and you are tracking it. I have learned the more you recognize and acknowledge, through gratitude, your loved one's efforts, the more signs and connections you receive. Not only is journaling important in the present to encourage signs and communications, and it's important for your future as well. I have found in the hours, days, or weeks when I struggled, coming back to the journal helped me tremendously. In times when I'm struggling now, going through down moments, or really in deep dark sadness, my journal is my light. Returning to all the signs and communication Roger has gifted me shines a bright light into my darkness. It focuses my attention back on the beauty of what I have, what we have, us. When I'm going deep into sadness because I think I'm missing something, the journal is a reflection that nothing is missing at all.

It grounds me and refocuses me on being thankful. How can I be in a place of darkness when I'm focusing on all Roger has done for me, on all he does for me every day to help illuminate my path. Journaling takes me to a place of love and peace.

It reminds us that our loved ones know our thoughts and our struggles, and therefore our needs. They want to help us succeed. They want us to want to be here and to feel as good as we can, so they put these wonderful nuggets and gifts in our path to keep us going, keep us wanting, keep us connecting. This is why journaling is so powerful. I take mine with me always. It's my wonderful reminder. As I reread my entries, I have caught connections and even more elements from the last two years, which makes it even more special.

Trust

Trust in all things related to the signs and communication from our loved ones is so important. Remember they always send positive messages. If you are seeing or interpreting something in a critical or negative way, that's your egoic mind interfering with the true message.

A few important things to know, or more accurately remember, about trust. The more you trust in the messages and communication, the more you will get. That is worth repeating: the more you trust the messages and communications you receive, the more you will get. The second most important thing is to trust your first instinct and feeling. What I mean here is your egoic mind has a bad habit of coming in and trying to ruin things by overthinking. Don't let it. If your first thought when you saw the blue jay was that it's a sign, that it's a nugget, then it was. If your first thought when you had a memory, when you saw a license plate, when a song came on, was that your loved one sent it, then that's what happened. If you have a visceral reaction, you feel it deep in your body like a ping that it was a sign from your loved one, trust it. It's so important because this foundational trust, this not questioning your deep knowing and intuition, is what lays the bricks for the road to a robust communication system between you and your loved one. The small signs — the birds, the numbers, the songs, someone says a certain thing to you in a certain way, and you immediately think of your loved one — recognizing and trusting these is the first step. It's building your language, your specific language with your loved one that is one hundred percent built on continuously trusting.

The more you trust, the faster you get at shutting down that egoic mind when it comes in and starts questioning. You may even get to a point where you laugh at your egoic mind when it tries to come in. You will be quicker and quicker at knowing and trusting, remembering what your soul already recognizes and knows deep within you.

Nature

Being in nature is healing in general. Just taking the opportunity to be outside is balancing and helps us connect with what is true and important. I have always been a runner, so being outdoors has always been a part of who I am. Hiking was an elevation of this; hiking in the mountains is an enchanted and inherently spiritual experience. You are one with what the universe has created and hiking in the mountains feels so freeing. None of the day-to-day burdens we tend to obsess over matter, and they fall away like they no longer exist.

At a soul level I have always known nature as my healing place. It's where I'm drawn. It allows me to listen to my inner voice, my intuition, to tap into God/ source in a quiet and still way. I have never listened to music while running or hiking. Roger and I had many deep discussions while navigating very difficult hikes.

When Roger passed, one of the things I was most drawn to do was take long walks. I walked and talked to him. I processed. I tuned in. I felt so much calmer walking. I had access to a great trail by me that went on for more than 20 miles. I started every day with a walk. I talked to Roger in those early days and felt a deep sense of him being with me on every walk. He was free from physical constraints and was with me, guiding me. As days progressed, I reserved portions of my walks to tap in and have silence; I devoted other portions to listening to spiritual content, audio books, podcasts, and affirmations. I always talked to Roger as I listened to audio spiritual content that resonated with me.

In the early days this time was a respite. I might cry, but I was free from that unbearable, paralyzing, deep grief. Somehow literally putting one foot in front of the other translated emotionally, as I started to transform my grief to see, feel, and deeply experience ways of connection. There are so many powerful elements to going on a walk when you're grieving. There is nature, there is movement, there is peace. Movement helps us see clearly; I always used my runs as a time to reflect on and digest issues or problems I was facing. It felt natural to spend this time with Roger, talking with him and asking for guidance as I tried to survive this unbearable, deep hurt in my heart.

These walks are part of each day for me. They are non-negotiable. Nowadays I start with a short affirmation that is specific to connection to my higher purpose, to God/source, and to truly knowing and feeling all is well. Combining this affirmation audibly while in the flow of my walk starts my day in a higher vibration. I have incorporated the walks and affirmations daily, and find this is my best time to listen to spiritual training or educational content maybe not originally intended for spirituality, but with clear underlying elements of learning and nuggets related to my journey. I am literally and metaphorically on a true spiritual journey.

Connection to nature has always been part of who I am, and it further assists with opening up our pathway to connect. Roger knows this is my best way for me to tap in, at least during waking hours. I envision it like I have an open door that he can easily (or at least more easily) come through to join me and connect with my thoughts.

Walking outside is the surest way to bring me back when I'm struggling, if I have been put in a situation or conversation or find myself triggered in a way where I feel like I can't climb out of the hole. When life throws me places that make me feel alone, in deep grief, overwhelmed or stressed, going outside for a walk brings me back. I can quickly get back to true knowing and a healthy state. Walking in nature grounds me regardless of my condition when I start. It is incredibly simple, but so powerful.

Positive In, Positive Out

In the last section on nature, I referenced daily affirmations. Affirmations can be extremely beneficial. You may want to experiment to discover what works best for you. I have found a few that are short that I rotate in the mornings. Seven to sixteen minutes of affirmation is perfect for me. I highly recommend using this to start your day. You set the tone of the day, as well as your intention. Setting your intentions for the day is important because it helps your mood and mental state, and focuses where you put your attention. Your intention equals your attention. I will state that another way: your daily intention equals your daily attention. It helps you start with a positive high vibe that allows you to connect with the other side with far more ease. It clears the negative clutter to open the door for you to see and recognize all of the amazing signs your loved ones are putting in your path. When you focus on the positive, you naturally vibe higher.

Two of my favorite affirmations are embodying your dream reality; one is a ten-minute affirmation track about seeing and feeling your dream reality, and the other is affirmations for a high vibration day. This second one is about eight minutes long and loops twice, essentially giving your brain muscle memory. Listening to these each day helps push out, override, and reset those negative thought patterns that can lead to dark feelings. You want tools in your arsenal to help you preempt as well as overcome these negative states.

Music

Music is a tool our loved ones use to get our attention and show us signs. And I don't just mean songs you recognize in connection with your loved one. Roger frequently uses my cell phone as a tool to get my attention, send me signs, and send me messages. I have had many songs pop up on my phone, songs I may never have heard and don't even know of the artist. When this happens, I know to pay special attention to the lyrics. Sometimes it's so obvious it's not necessary to give it special attention. One day I had been thinking that the soft whispers of touch I often feel on my face or hand while meditating or visualizing could possibly be Roger kissing me. Later that day a song randomly popped up on my phone titled "Ghostly Kisses;" the lyrics were completely and totally validating, and confirmed a few weeks later by a medium.

If you hear a song and the lyrics resonate or connect to a thought or a conversation or even a question you may have asked your loved one on the other side, know songs are a powerful tool they can use to give you information or validation. Songs can link us in many ways. We may play our loved one's favorite song as a way to connect as well. We can use music to knock on the door for a visit or ask permission to connect; it's another way to open the pathway.

Music is such a powerful influence on our emotions, so it has an amazing soul tapping ability to connect us with our essence. As I write this, I just experienced the whisper on my right cheek, a soft brush on my face, a kiss of hello, a confirmation as Roger helps guide me to try and assist others in ways to connect.

Mediums

Mediums can be a powerful and amazing resource for connecting with your loved ones. I won't spend too much time on it because there are awesome resources dedicated specifically to choosing a medium, which I will provide at the end, but finding one that is legit and trustworthy is so important. I do not recommend engaging a medium who has not been vetted and validated. The best mediums have been through extremely intensive certification and training programs that include double- and triple-blind verifications and testing. Going to a great medium is such a beautiful and phenomenal experience you don't want to dilute it with a bad one. There are several organizations that test and verify mediums with online contact list like the Forever Family Foundation (FFF) and the Windbridge Institute. Both are great resources.

I will outline when and how I have personally found it most powerful to see a medium. I have been to several and have had amazing mediums drawn into my path for unscheduled readings. All have been game changing experiences with powerful takeaways. All have been certified mediums.

Seeing a medium as you start your journey can be very powerful. Trust your intuition on timing. If you are too raw or the deep grief is just too fresh, you may want to wait a bit. I had my first reading about seven months after Roger's passing. The timing for me was meant to be, although a little sooner would have been fine. Really great mediums tend to be booked at least three to six months in advance, some as much as a year. I reached out to my first medium about four months prior to being able to schedule the reading.

The reading for me was an hour with Roger, with validating information through the medium. This is exactly what, on a soul level, I was expecting. I got all ready just like I always did to see Roger in the physical world. One of the most powerful aspects was just confirming my intuitive knowing. The medium validated what I knew to be the large signs from Roger. He validated that Roger was listening to my thoughts as I spoke to him in my mind. He brought up multiple really big things that I had only told Roger in my thoughts. He brought up people, events, and happenings around and following Roger's passing that are not known to anyone. He brought up elements of Roger's childhood that were not known or known by very few. It was a very beautiful and emotional experience. Because these readings tend to be very intense emotional experiences, I recommend recording the session if the medium allows it. I went back and listened several times and after each one I caught things that were meaningful that I did not catch live. Several were references the medium thought Roger was using to describe or set context, but which were actually meaningful elements or symbols. You also want to block out an hour or so after a reading. With the emotional intensity of a reading, you can either be on a mega high or super tired or both.

When choosing a medium, think of how they would match or vibe with the energy of your loved one on the other side. For instance, I knew within seconds of my first reading that the medium's personality and energy would be very much in vibration with Roger. On the other hand, I was at an event with a medium who had a very strong personality — extremely loud, flamboyant, and dominant in nature. I knew Roger would not want to use this medium as a conduit. The person was not a fit for Roger (or me).

When you have an appointment, set your intention that morning. It is important to talk to your loved one ahead of time and set the intention; ask for them to come through. You may even want to ask them to mention something specific during the reading. Chances are they will validate the conversation you have with them pre appointment regardless. I had a medium ask me if I had changed clothes several times the morning of the appointment. I had and had been talking to Roger while doing it so he mentioned this through her as validation. Validation not just of her ability to communicate between us but also confirmation he is always with me.

Mediums can provide a great foundation for you to start learning or validating your language with your loved one. They may mention signs you were slightly unclear about, which will help you hear more from your loved ones. The more you see and hear, the more you will be able to see and hear. Once you have recognizable signs and communication, it continues to get stronger and build. I recommend seeing a medium early in your process to help set the foundation and build that trust in your communication.

After you've built communication and you feel you have a strong connection and language, you may want to consider a reading to tie everything together. At this point, a reading can be really helpful and confirm you're on the right path. This is a time when additional layers of your spiritual journey may peek through on a reading as well. I view this second type of reading as icing. You've built the cake, you've baked the cake, and the medium helps you put the icing on it, tying everything together and helping with all of your knowing. This can quiet your egoic mind and further your ability to trust your intuition.

A third opportunity to enlist the help of a medium is around a large or significant event. An upcoming event, memory, or holiday are powerful times to get the help of a medium. It can help ease anxiety or validate your loved one's presence. Mediums often bring in elements from your guides or theirs. You may learn elements of your soul's purpose or at least related nuggets of information that can help you understand and come to terms with the why. This information can also help you keep going and easily open doors.

I have learned that my soul has responsibilities to others, to the collective, so I have to do my part. The reward of my work and diligence now is eternity with the love of all my lifetimes once my work here is complete. That helps me keep going. That and the amazing love and gifts Roger showers me with each and every day. I just need to do my part as a partner in this union as a soul navigating this lifetime.

Akashic Records

For those not familiar with Akashic Records, the term Akashic goes back to the late 1800s and is an ancient Sanskrit word. The direct translation is ether, luminous, or space. The Akashic Records are known to be a compilation of events, emotions, experiences, encoding, recorded in a non-physical space known as the astral plane. The Akashic Records hold your soul's records.

Our soul's records from all our lifetimes connect or are tied to our current life in the physical world.

The Akashic Records can be a place to tap into to really understand your work and path. Doing Akashic work, especially led by a trained healer in the space, can be an amazingly rewarding experience. The work can help you heal traumas from this lifetime, as well as from past lifetimes. You may be carrying trauma, experiences, or feelings that need to be released. These traumas can go from one lifetime to the next. This includes and can be inclusive of experiences of grief and perceived loss. Maybe you had a trauma in a past life where you left your loved one early or your loved one transitioned and left you feeling lost or alone. This work can, and in my experience does, help with great healing, which can be a door opener or a pathway to finding joy again.

I found Akashic work beneficial for a slightly different reason. For me, the healing nature of Akashic work inherently helped open me up. It helped clear the pathway to receive communication and signs. The work felt healing and peaceful to my heart, to my soul, which I so desperately needed. I was in such unbearably deep pain. It let me see glimpses of a path forward where Roger and I were still and forever connected, a path where he could continue to support and guide me. A path that, along with my free will, could help me realize and fulfill my potential. A path of understanding why this had to happen, and why it had to happen when it did. It helped me release the why and feel into the how, the how I/we move forward. How our union continues. How our union is in no way diminished with a change of physical representation. It showed me validation, it showed me the path I was on of trust, how I trust in my deep sense of knowing, of oneness with our relationship.

I had never heard of Akashic Records. I had no knowledge of healers or spiritual coaches doing this work, but one found her way onto my path.

I reached out, knowing on some level I was being called to work with her, that she was meant to help with my grief, to be part of my path going forward. The first session was just to get to know each other, see if it was a good fit for both of us. Her energy immediately felt deeply right. I knew this was where I was meant to be. Working with my Akashic Records through my spiritual coach was full of many firsts, opening doors to many unknowns, yet it felt comforting. I never was afraid, even though it was a total unknown to me. I looked forward to our work, to the sessions, and the peace afterwards. There was a meditative and calming nature about the work for me. She let me record them, which I found very helpful. We set the intention for each session based on what I was feeling, the challenges or needs I specifically had at that time. She consulted her guides prior to each session as well. Some sessions were chakra based where I had big needs and big pain. One of my recordings is specifically around that work. When I listen to the recordings, I pick the one that is calling to me.

I'm not sure of others' experiences as it pertains to grief, but I know the testimonials of my coach and famous experts in this space are awesome. The results are life changing, awe inspiring, and let you see with a new level of clarity.

It was perfect divine timing for me to go through this process. People say grief can be a block. I envision it like a dark cloud. My Akashic work helped shine a light through the dark cloud, to help me further see the path to Roger, to our deep connection. I cried a lot going into that first session, explaining our love and all that we had been through, my grief and his illness. The session was beautiful and gave me my first feeling of peace following Roger's transition. The work was such an amazing gift. The messages that came through in and around my sessions tied strongly with those I received directly. I am so thankful for the gift that work has brought to us; not just me, but us.

Spiritual Coach

Akashic work, if you decide to go that route, may bring you a spiritual coach, but you may choose to find a coach outside of Akashic work as well. Early on, in the first year or two, as you explore your awakening, a coach can be very helpful. You may be drawn to having a guide and want to keep a coach. I have approached my deep spiritual awakening the way I have always approached my life. I love learning. I love exploring all elements of a new area, coming at it from multiple angles, going deep into the areas that resonate most with me. I have found this with my spiritual learning as well. You will see from my suggested reading list I have taken a diverse approach. I have found that there are phenomenal lessons and learnings in places, books, and teachings that are not traditionally spiritual.

A coach who has explored many aspects of spirituality, connectedness, soul purpose, and work on how to do "human" in this lifetime may really help you. It may help you explore and figure out areas of interest and growth, and it may show you more quickly areas that don't resonate with you. This will allow you to save your energy and focus on things that feel good for you. Working with a coach may also speed up your healing time. Opening new doors and discovering elements of healing may take longer alone.

The most important aspect of finding and choosing someone to work with is picking someone who resonates with your energy. You should feel good about your work together; you should look forward to and feel comfort and ease in your sessions. You should have a knowing that working with this person is helping you stay true to your soul's path. You may find that the universe and your loved ones put people on your path to help you with aspects of your growth. I am a firm believer in divine timing and guidance. For me this meant finding just the right podcast or book or series that ultimately introduced me to healers and coaches I was ready to call in.

It's important to find someone who is positive. Whether it's God based, if that is what is meaningful to you, or connects with angels or connects to or represents the source and source energy, you should be getting healing, positive energy. The coach is just a conduit to help you with the process.

Past Life Regression

I always had a sense that Roger and I had known each other before we met. When we met in this lifetime there was an immediate sense of recognition, we already seemed to completely know each other and ourselves as a couple. It was like this instant download of knowing all the most important deep truths about each other and this immediate knowing that this was it, this is what our hearts and souls had been searching for. Because of this, even though I hadn't given it conscious thought, I also found an interest in past life work. Once Roger passed, I knew there was more to the depth of our immediate connection. After starting the Akashic work I became very interested in tying this together.

Deep down I knew we had been together in countless lifetimes before. I knew this for myself. Over the year following his passing I had this validated many ways. After Roger passed, I reread beautiful love letters he wrote me when we were dating. In them he spoke of our connection and his knowing as soon as we met in this lifetime that I was the girl he dreamed of when he was a boy. I firmly believe those dreams were a remembering, a recognition of each other from our past lives. It kept coming up for me, in my knowing, in my messages from Roger. Then I scheduled a reading with a medium who referred to our past lives together.

About 10 months later I had a medium who read me "randomly" out of a group. She started the reading not with the traditional "you have a husband on the other side" or "you have spouse energy" or "a man of your generation or a contemporary is coming through." She started the reading by looking at me and saying: "Half your heart and half your soul is on the other side." I could not have felt this more completely, accurately, or deeply. She said Roger and I had spent many lifetimes together. She then said she had good news and bad news. The bad news was I had to stick out this lifetime because I had big purpose. The good news was I/we never have to do this again. We would never lose each other again after this; we are together infinitely on the other side. I let out the most visceral "thank God." I felt what she said with every cell of my being. She went on to mention many hundreds of lifetimes we were together and some details around them which were very interesting because they connect specifically to elements of our being together in this lifetime. I knew then I needed to go deeper with the work.

This reading occurred only a few weeks after I had experienced my first hypnosis, which was specifically for past life regression. The work was so validating and all made sense as to why we were drawn to certain things in this lifetime. For example, our love of the west, mountains, hiking, nature, horses, and dogs. We had a gorgeous horse farm out west in a previous lifetime. This work tied so many elements of this lifetime together, made so much sense. It tied together things I felt during my larger awakening, things I and we felt our entire relationship and that my soul knew.

In another regression, I was taken back to a lifetime where Roger and I had this beautiful little house in the country. On a very pretty piece of land, surrounded by trees. The perfect, quaint house with a pretty little porch. I watched our interaction together from within and with out, as if it were a movie, I was in but also witnessing. During this lifetime I was able to watch as I delivered a baby, a little girl via a mid-wife in the home. With Roger by my side, I was looking deep in the baby's eyes and sobbing. There was such a deep connection words cannot do justice to, I felt it with every fiber in me. My therapist asked as I walked through the scene to look at the baby and tell me her name, I said Isabella, we call her Bella, through my intense tears.

If you have questions about your past lives and connections, regression could be a great tool. If you really don't have questions, but just want another layer of confirmation or even just deeper insight, this is wonderful work. During my regressions I was able to experience in our past lifetimes — to see, walk through, and feel with all the emotion, with total presence. I found the work very powerful. I also found that my heart completely led the way. There were times while in a regressed state I was just quietly sobbing, experiencing, more accurately remembering, all of our beautiful lives.

The last thing I will mention about past life regressions is that I had a knowing after Roger passed in this lifetime that I was feeling the deep pain and weight of the loss of him from many, many lifetimes layered on top of each other. The work I did with past life regressions further validated this deep feeling within me.

Sample Day

As you dive into your path, your deeper awakening, and connections, let your heart and intuition guide you. Some of the tools I have discussed may resonate for you, some may not. You may find other tools I have not discussed that are specific and very meaningful to your journey. There are so many amazing tools available. No matter what spiritual tools, practices, or programs resonate, the most important thing is learning what works best for you, so that you have them as anchors or tools in your toolbox. This is particularly important for your daily practice, as well as when you really need them to guide you back. Like breadcrumbs in the forest, let these tools guide you home when you need it most.

In this section, I will lay out what I do in a typical day as my daily practice.

Morning

Following a short walk with my dogs, one of the first things I do before looking at email, social media, etc., is to listen to fourteen minutes of affirmations on embodying my dream reality. I sometimes rotate in a sixteen-minute affirmation on having a high vibration day. Both have positive messages about connecting with the source and embodying my highest self.

I start my morning with a nice walk. Unless there is lightning, it's almost always outside. I love starting my day in nature. I have set my intention for the day with my affirmations and following that I often start a walk listening to them with a clear and open mind; being open to receive is very important for me. I believe movement helps unblock and de-stress us, making it easier to connect and listen to your intuition. I like to walk four miles or so in the morning, but 30 minutes will really help support your practice.

Day

I usually work during the day, but if it's a tough workday or I'm experiencing triggers, I may go for a walk around the block to reground myself between meetings. On weekends, I listen to an audio book related to my spiritual journey or a podcast from my list in the recommended tools section. Another tool I use is a simple mantra, "I am enough. I have enough." Or "I am divinely guided, and I am divinely protected." These are great to repeat to yourself often, especially if you're feeling down or thinking negative thoughts.

Pre-Bed Routine

Meditation is one of my go tos every night, even if it's only four minutes. No matter where I am or what time I meditate, it is always a game changer for me. I start by getting completely ready for bed so I can end my night with my meditation and go to sleep. I added something new about a year ago, so the year after Roger transitioned, that feels powerful to me. I purchased a mist that I spray above me into the air as I mentally or verbally set my intention. My intention is always to connect with Roger. I use the spray before meditating so I have a fresh woodsy smell surrounding me. I have since learned since I spray the mist above my head it helps activate my 3rd eye which is instrumental in connecting across the veil. For me there is a deep knowing that engaging the senses helps open me for connection as well. For the actual meditation, I have used meditation apps off and on. If you find one that works for you, great. If it's a guided meditation, I personally prefer the ones with subtle noise, such as singing bowls or waves in the background. Some of the guided meditations on *Simple Habit* are really nice and layer in visualization, which I find very powerful. I recently found a great one that offers a variety of meditation and movement practices to help you relax and tune in called Open. The offer some great virtual events including sound baths.

Three-minute Meditation

Every night I listen to a chanting meditation from Jay Shetty's audio book, *Think Like a Monk*. The audio is great. Part three has a three-minute section of chanting meditation that I love. Chanting is a powerful way to meditate because you engage your voice as well as your mind. Your throat chakra can be a powerful tool for manifestation. I find people who struggle with silent meditation do really well with chanting, which can be a great gateway form of meditation to get you started. The newer app Open has great meditations as well, all different lengths. They also have great sound baths and other listening sessions that are very helpful.

Five-minute Visualization

I follow the three-minute chanting meditation with a five-minute visualization. I have a few places Roger and I visited over the years that are my favorites and connect to nature. I pick one for my visualization, and the visualization puts me right there with Roger. I take myself through the total experience of being there, using all the senses — touching, smelling, talking, truly feeling his face on mine, the light stubble of his beard as it grew from the day, really feeling into all the details. What he's wearing, what I'm wearing, the emotions we are feeling, being one hundred percent in those moments. Visualization is a powerful tool for us to call in our loved ones. We are asking for them to join us and it's a wonderful way to connect.

Most nights I pull an Oracle card, asking Roger and/or God/ the source for insights into the next day; or I may ask a specific question. I pull one card and I find they are always purposeful.

Bed

Gratitude

GRATITUDE IS HOW I TRANSITION TO SLEEP. I TALK TO ROGER AND thank him every single night for all of the gifts, blessings, and signs he brings to me. I express thanks for our amazing connection and relationship. I always set an intention in my gratitude prayer: "I open myself up to receive you." Then I generally thank God, my angels, and my loved ones on the other side, as well as my spirit team for helping guide me on this journey and helping us stay so connected. I thank God for specific blessings from the day or week. I also thank God for the signs, information, and downloads from my spirit team, loved ones and all who walk and represent God's love and light. This allows me to be open to receive any and all positive messages or information. You have free will so if you are open for help and signs you have to let God / the universe know that. I end with a quick visualization, an image in my mind's eye, often with my eyes open. I see Roger, then I express my love for him and drift off.

Journal

I always have a journal along with a pen close by at night. I find it important to try and write down visitation dream details as soon as I wake. I journal the details before falling back to sleep so I don't lose anything important.

When you journal in the night, you have it to review when you wake. You have captured at least the main details, which may help trigger other important elements you think of in the morning. I also write down the date and time of the visit, as I find tracking times and trends is helpful. If I wake in the middle of the night and I'm unaware of a visit or don't think we have had one yet, I will ask if Roger to please come visit me. I may even ask for something specific, like I really want to hug him or kiss him. I have found this helps and he delivers, which makes me feel so loved and blessed.

Going in and out of a relaxed dream state is the perfect time to ask for a visit because we are in our most receptive state. Journaling is important so you don't miss or lose details that might be symbolic that require a bit of marination. In addition, if you have more than one visit in a night the journal will help you with clarifying details from each one. For instance, for me one visit might be related to information / knowledge that is relevant to our company and the second might be deeply personal and important for my heart.

Conclusion

I hope our story and this book help open you to the realm of the possible. Some elements may resonate strongly with you, and some may not. You may want to experiment with the elements that call to you. I did. These were the tools and routines I found most beneficial. In the final section I list some of my go-to tools and recommendations.

In many ways we have been given an amazing gift. We are no longer physically limited by time and space to be with our loved ones. They are always present with us and can show up and guide us as much as we are open to receiving them. They are no longer constrained by physical limitations and our relationship is no longer bound by the limits of the human world. Open yourself to the beautiful magic they so want to provide.

Love and Light,
Lindsay (& Roger ♡)

Resource Guide

Books

1. *Broken Horses* by Brandi Carlile
2. *Daring Greatly* by Brene Brown
3. *Greenlights* by Matthew McConaughey
4. *The Alchemist* by Paulo Coelho
5. *The Light Between Us* by Laura Lynn Jackson
6. *Recapture the Rapture* by Jamie Wheel
7. *Signs* by Laura Lynn Jackson
8. *Spirited* by Rebecca Rosen
9. *Think Like a Monk* by Jay Shetty*
10. *The Power of Positive Thinking* by Norman Vincent Peale*
11. *The Seat of the Soul* by Gary Zukav*
12. *The 5 Second Rule* by Mel Robbins*
13. *The Secret* by Rhona Byrne
14. *Universal Human* by Gary Zukav
15. *Untamed* by Glennon Doyal
16. *Untethered Soul* by Michael Singer
17. *Your Soul Purpose* by Kim Russo

Podcasts

1. *Affirmations for Spiritual Health and Well-Being* by Christina
2. *Angels and Awakenings,* Julie Jancius
3. *A Psychic's Story* Nichole Bigley
4. *Bewildered* with Martha Beck
5. *Divine Downloads,* Cassandra Bodzak
6. *Grieving Voices* Victoria Volk
7. *Highest Self Podcast,* Sahara Rose
8. *Intuitive Souls* Erica Russo
9. *The Mindvalley Podcast* with Vishen Lakhiani
10. *We Can Do Hard Things,* Glennon Doyle

Websites/Newsletters/Organizations

1. *The Awakened Way* – Suzanne Giesemann (beautiful and powerful daily messages)
2. Forever Family Foundation (foreverfamilyfoundation.org) – Certified mediums, grief retreats, radio show (amazing resource)
3. Orphanwisdom.com by Stephen Jenkinson (he is brilliant, so much powerful messaging)
4. *The Shift Network* (theshiftnetwork.com) – phenomenal online courses, events and content
5. Soulproof.com by Mark Pitstick
6. Yoursoulsplan.com by Rob Swartz

Meditation

1. *Headspace*
2. *Think Like a Monk* chanting meditation

3. *Simple Habit*
4. *OPEN app*
5. Use Singing bowls

Mediums

1. Forever Family Foundation (foreverfamilyfoundation.org). My specific experience:
   a. Amy Utsman
   b. Joe Perreta
   c. Joanne Gerber
   d. Joe Shiel
   e. Kim Russo (may no longer take appointments)
   f. Renee Buck
   g. Julie Jancius

Past Life Regression

1. Rob Schwartz (yoursoulsplan.com)
2. Steve Shields – Keystone Healing Center (Chicago)

Programs/Communities

1. Alina Grayson (alignedhabits.com) – great coaching programs for leaning into your soul's purpose and power, very spiritually driven programs; she runs her business off Facebook, so best to message her on FB or Instagram alinagraysoncoaching
2. Angel Membership (theangelmedium.com) – Julie Jancius (excellent programs and community for helping you on your intuitive journey)
3. Cassandra Bodzak – (cassandrabodzak.com)

Akashic Guide:

1. Arti Pancholi (Facebook or Insta arti-pancholi)
2. Linda Howe (lindahowe.com)

Other Helpful Tools

1. A mini alter (great spot for your meditation and mindfulness practice – sacred space)
2. Baths with bath bombs, Epsom salts, scents, or candles can relax you and help you connect.
3. Breath work
4. Consistent routines for bed. This helps you sleep better and deeper, helping you connect.
5. Crystals
6. Having a grounding mantra to repeat when you are stressed, down, or just need a little help. My go to is: "I am divinely guided and divinely protected."
7. Images — looking at photos of your loved one when you wake and before you go to bed. Great tool right before visualization or meditation, as well.
8. Sound healing
9. Singing bowls
10. Yoga (restorative)
11. Shamans
12. Reiki/energy healing
13. Scented sprays that connect with nature or smells that make you feel really good. Forest Spirit is my favorite (kejiwastore.com/).
14. Sacred journal — journaling is such an important tool. I highly recommend a sacred journal for signs and visitation notes.

Printed in the United States
by Baker & Taylor Publisher Services